vegetarian
...made simple

This edition published in 2011
LOVE FOOD is an imprint of Parragon Books Ltd

Parragon
Queen Street House
4 Queen Street
Bath BA1 1HE, UK

ISBN: 978-1-4454-3058-4

Printed in China

Produced by Ivy Contract
Photography by Charlie Paul

Notes for the Reader

This book uses imperial, metric, or US cup measurements. Follow the same units of measurement through-out; do not mix imperial and metric. All spoon measurements are level: teaspoons are assumed to be 5 ml, and tablespoons are assumed to be 15 ml. Unless otherwise stated, milk is assumed to be full fat, eggs and individual vegetables are medium, and pepper is freshly ground black pepper.

The times given are an approximate guide only. Preparation times differ according to the techniques used by different people and the cooking times may also vary from those given. Optional ingredients, variations or serving suggestions have not been included in the calculations.

Recipes using raw or very lightly cooked eggs should be avoided by infants, the elderly, pregnant women, convalescents, and anyone suffering from an illness. Pregnant and breastfeeding women are advised to avoid eating peanuts and peanut products. Sufferers from nut allergies should be aware that some of the ready-made ingredients used in the recipes in this book may contain nuts. Always check the packaging before use. Vegetarians should be aware that some of the ready-made ingredients used in the recipes in this book may contain animal products. Always check the packaging before use.

vegetarian

introduction

Following a vegetarian diet was once considered to be rather eccentric and certainly very dull! However, in recent years more and more people have chosen to embrace a meat-free diet, for a number of reasons. The most obvious of these is a desire not to eat animals or fish, but health issues often come into the equation, too—for example, sufferers of irritable bowel syndrome often find that meat is one of the triggers for the symptoms. Meat and fish can also be expensive, so even non-vegetarians often choose to have two or three meat-free meals each week.

The really good news is that the ever-increasing interest in vegetarianism has raised its profile in the world of gastronomy. Chefs have risen to the challenge with skill and enthusiasm and have come up with some truly creative recipes—and the meat-free diet is no longer dull!

If you are new to vegetarianism, it is important to remember that you cannot simply exclude meat and fish from your usual recipes, because this will deprive you of protein and other vital nutrients that are essential to your health and wellbeing. Meat and fish must be replaced with other protein- and nutrient-rich foods such as beans, nuts and seeds, bean curd, and dairy products. If you have allergies to any of these foods, take advice from your doctor or a nutritionist to ensure that you will not damage your health instead of enhancing it.

Whether you are planning to be a "proper" vegetarian, or you are having vegetarian guests to dinner, or you just want to ring the changes and have an occasional meal without meat, there are some fabulous ideas in this book, taken from around the world. For the best results, choose really fresh, top-quality ingredients—this will ensure that you get the maximum goodness out of your food, as well as superb flavor.

Have fun experimenting!

light meals & starters

cracked marinated olives

ingredients

serves 8

1 lb/450 g can or jar unpitted large
    green olives, drained
4 garlic cloves, peeled
2 tsp coriander seeds
1 small lemon
4 sprigs of fresh thyme
4 feathery stalks of fennel
2 small fresh red chiles (optional)
pepper
Spanish extra-virgin olive oil,
    to cover
slices of fresh crusty bread,
    to serve

method

1 To allow the flavors of the marinade to penetrate the olives, place the olives on a cutting board and, using a rolling pin, bash them lightly so that they crack slightly. Alternatively, use a sharp knife to cut a lengthwise slit in each olive as far as the pit. Using the flat side of a broad knife, lightly crush each garlic clove. Using a mortar and pestle, crack the coriander seeds. Cut the lemon, with its rind, into small chunks.

2 Put the olives, garlic, coriander seeds, lemon chunks, thyme sprigs, fennel, and chiles, if using, in a large bowl and toss together. Season with pepper, but you should not need to add salt as preserved olives are usually salty enough. Pack the ingredients tightly into a glass jar with a lid. Pour in enough olive oil to cover the olives, then seal the jar tightly.

3 Let the olives stand at room temperature for 24 hours, then marinate in the refrigerator for at least 1 week but preferably 2 weeks before serving. From time to time, gently give the jar a shake to remix the ingredients. Return the olives to room temperature and remove from the oil to serve. Provide toothpicks for spearing the olives. Serve with slices of fresh crusty bread.

salted almonds

ingredients

serves 6–8

8 oz/225 g/scant 1½ cups whole
 almonds, in their skins or
 blanched (see method)
4 tbsp Spanish olive oil
coarse sea salt
1 tsp paprika or ground cumin
 (optional)

method

1 Fresh almonds in their skins are superior in taste, but blanched almonds are much more convenient. If the almonds are not blanched, put them in a bowl, cover with boiling water for 3–4 minutes, then plunge them into cold water for 1 minute. Drain them well in a sieve, then slide off the skins between your fingers. Dry the almonds well on paper towels.

2 Put the olive oil in a roasting pan and swirl it round so that it covers the bottom. Add the almonds and toss them in the pan so that they are evenly coated in the oil, then spread them out in a single layer.

3 Roast the almonds in a preheated oven, 350°F/180°C, for 20 minutes, or until they are light golden brown, tossing several times during the cooking. Drain the almonds on paper towels, then transfer them to a bowl.

4 While the almonds are still warm, sprinkle with plenty of sea salt and the paprika or cumin, if using, and toss well together to coat. Serve the almonds warm or cold. The almonds are at their best when served freshly cooked, so, if possible, cook them on the day that you plan to eat them. However, they can be stored in an airtight container for up to 3 days.

hummus

ingredients

serves 8

8 oz/225 g/1⅓ cups dried
    chickpeas, covered with water
    and soaked overnight
juice of 2 large lemons
5 fl oz/150 ml/⅔ cup sesame
    seed paste
2 garlic cloves, crushed
4 tbsp extra virgin olive oil
small pinch of ground cumin
salt and pepper
1 tsp paprika
chopped flat-leaf parsley,
    to garnish
pita bread, to serve

method

1 Drain the chickpeas, put in a saucepan, and cover with
    cold water. Bring to the boil then let simmer for about
    2 hours, until very tender.

2 Drain the chickpeas, reserving a little of the liquid,
    and put in a food processor, reserving a few to garnish.
    Blend the chickpeas until smooth, gradually adding
    the lemon juice and enough reserved liquid to form
    a smooth, thick purée.

3 Add the sesame seed paste, garlic, 3 tablespoons of
    the olive oil, and the cumin and blend until smooth.
    Season with salt and pepper.

4 Turn the mixture into a shallow serving dish and chill
    in the refrigerator for 2–3 hours before serving.

5 To serve, mix the reserved olive oil with the paprika
    and drizzle over the top of the dish. Sprinkle with the
    parsley and the reserved chickpeas. Accompany with
    warm pita bread.

guacamole

ingredients

serves 4

2 large, ripe avocados
juice of 1 lime, or to taste
2 tsp olive oil
½ onion, finely chopped
1 fresh green chile, such as
    poblano, seeded and
    finely chopped
1 garlic clove, crushed
¼ tsp ground cumin
1 tbsp chopped fresh cilantro,
    plus extra leaves to garnish
    (optional)
salt and pepper

method

1 Cut the avocados in half lengthwise and twist the
   2 halves in opposite directions to separate. Stab
   the pit with the point of a sharp knife and lift out.

2 Peel, then coarsely chop, the avocado halves and place
   in a nonmetallic bowl. Squeeze over the lime juice and
   add the oil.

3 Mash the avocados with a fork until the desired
   consistency is reached—either chunky or smooth.
   Blend in the onion, chile, garlic, cumin, and chopped
   cilantro, then season with salt and pepper.

4 Transfer to a serving dish and serve at once, to avoid
   discoloration, garnished with the cilantro leaves,
   if liked.

eggplant pâté

ingredients

serves 4–6

2 large eggplants
4 tbsp extra virgin olive oil
2 garlic cloves, very finely chopped
4 tbsp lemon juice
salt and pepper
6 crisp breads, to serve

method

1 Score the skins of the eggplants with the point of a sharp knife, without piercing the flesh, and place them on a baking sheet. Bake in a preheated oven, 350°F/180°C, for 1¼ hours, or until soft.

2 Remove the eggplants from the oven and leave until cool enough to handle. Cut them in half and, using a spoon, scoop out the flesh into a bowl. Mash the flesh thoroughly.

3 Gradually beat in the olive oil then stir in the garlic and lemon juice. Season with salt and pepper to taste. Cover with plastic wrap and store in the refrigerator until required. Serve with the crisp breads.

borscht

ingredients

serves 6

1 onion
2 oz/55 g/¼ cup butter
12 oz/350 g raw beets, cut into
  thin sticks, and 1 raw beet,
  grated
1 carrot, cut into thin sticks
3 celery stalks, thinly sliced
2 tomatoes, peeled, seeded
  and chopped
6¼ cups vegetable stock
1 tbsp white wine vinegar
1 tbsp sugar
2 large fresh dill sprigs
4 oz/115 g white cabbage,
  shredded
salt and pepper
5 fl oz/150 ml/ ⅔ cup sour cream,
  to garnish

method

1 Slice the onion into rings. Melt the butter in a large, heavy-bottom pan. Add the onion and cook over low heat, stirring occasionally, for 3–5 minutes, or until softened. Add the sticks of beet, carrot, celery, and chopped tomatoes and cook, stirring frequently, for 4–5 minutes.

2 Add the stock, vinegar, and sugar, and snip a tablespoon of dill into the pan. Season to taste with salt and pepper. Bring to a boil, reduce the heat and simmer for 35–40 minutes, or until the vegetables are tender.

3 Stir in the cabbage, cover, and simmer for 10 minutes, then stir in the grated beet, with any juices, and cook for an additional 10 minutes. Ladle the borscht into warmed bowls. Garnish with sour cream and another tablespoon of snipped dill and serve.

vegetable soup with pesto

ingredients

serves 4

32 fl oz/1 liter/4 cups cold water
bouquet garni of 1 fresh parsley
     sprig, 1 fresh thyme sprig, and
     1 bay leaf, tied together with
     clean string
2 celery stalks, chopped
3 baby leeks, chopped
4 baby carrots, chopped
5½ oz/150 g new potatoes,
     scrubbed and cut into chunks
4 tbsp shelled fava beans
     or peas
6 oz/175 g canned cannellini
     or flageolet beans, drained
     and rinsed
3 heads bok choy
5½ oz/150 g/generous
     3¼ cups arugula
pepper

pesto

2 large handfuls fresh basil leaves
1 fresh green chile, seeded
2 garlic cloves
4 tbsp olive oil
1 tsp finely grated Parmesan
     cheese

method

1 Put the water and bouquet garni into a large pan and add the celery, leeks, carrots, and potatoes. Bring to a boil, then reduce the heat and let simmer for 10 minutes.

2 Stir in the fava beans or peas and canned beans and let simmer for an additional 10 minutes. Stir in the bok choy and arugula, season with pepper and let simmer for an additional 2–3 minutes. Remove and discard the bouquet garni.

3 Meanwhile, to make the pesto, put the basil, chile, garlic, and oil into a food processor and pulse to form a thick paste. Stir in the cheese.

4 Stir most of the pesto into the soup, then ladle into warmed bowls. Top with the remaining pesto and serve at once.

watercress soup

ingredients

serves 4

2 bunches of watercress
   (approx 7 oz/200 g),
   thoroughly cleaned
3 tbsp butter
2 onions, chopped
8 oz/225 g potatoes, peeled
   and roughly chopped
40 fl oz/1.25 liters/5 cups
   vegetable stock or water
salt and pepper
whole nutmeg, for grating
   (optional)
4 fl oz/125 ml/½ cup crème
   fraîche, yogurt, or sour cream

method

1 Remove the leaves from the stalks of the watercress
   and keep on one side. Roughly chop the stalks.

2 Melt the butter in a large pan over medium heat,
   add the onion, and cook for 4–5 minutes until soft.
   Do not brown.

3 Add the potato to the pan and mix well with the onion.
   Add the watercress stalks and the stock. Bring to a boil,
   then reduce the heat, cover, and simmer for 15–20
   minutes until the potato is soft.

4 Add the watercress leaves and stir in to heat through.
   Remove from the heat and use a hand-held stick
   blender to process the soup until smooth. Alternatively,
   pour the soup into a blender, process until smooth,
   and return to the rinsed-out pan. Reheat and season
   with salt and pepper, adding a good grating of
   nutmeg, if using.

5 Serve in warm bowls with the crème fraîche spooned
   on top.

white bean soup

ingredients

serves 4

6 oz/175 g/³/₄ cup dried cannellini
　　beans, soaked in cold water
　　to cover overnight
48 fl oz/1.5 liters/6 cups
　　vegetable stock
4 oz/115 g dried corallini,
　　conchigliette piccole,
　　or other soup pasta
6 tbsp olive oil
2 garlic cloves, finely chopped
4 tbsp chopped fresh
　　flat-leaf parsley
salt and pepper
fresh crusty bread, to serve

method

1 Drain the soaked beans and place them in a large,
heavy-bottom pan. Add the stock and bring to a boil.
Partially cover the pan, then reduce the heat, and let
simmer for 2 hours, or until tender.

2 Transfer about half the beans and a little of the stock
to a food processor or blender and process to a smooth
purée. Return the purée to the pan and stir well to mix.
Return the soup to a boil.

3 Add the pasta to the soup, return to a boil, and cook
for 10 minutes, or until tender.

4 Meanwhile, heat 4 tablespoons of the olive oil in
a small pan. Add the garlic and cook over low heat,
stirring frequently, for 4–5 minutes, or until golden. Stir
the garlic into the soup and add the parsley. Season
with salt and pepper and ladle into warmed soup
bowls. Drizzle with the remaining olive oil and serve
immediately with crusty bread.

chinese mushroom soup

ingredients

serves 4

½ oz/15 g dried Chinese wood
    ear mushrooms
4 oz/115 g dried thin Chinese
    egg noodles
2 tsp arrowroot or cornstarch
32 fl oz/1 liter/4 cups vegetable
    stock
2-inch/5-cm piece fresh ginger,
    peeled and sliced
2 tbsp dark soy sauce
2 tsp mirin or sweet sherry
1 tsp rice vinegar
4 small bok choy, each cut in half
salt and pepper
snipped fresh Chinese or ordinary
    chives, to garnish

method

1 Put the dried wood ear mushrooms in a heatproof
bowl and pour over enough boiling water to cover,
then let stand for 20 minutes, or until the mushrooms
are tender. Meanwhile, boil the noodles for 3 minutes,
or according to the package instructions, until soft.
Drain well and rinse with cold water to stop the
noodles cooking, and set aside.

2 Strain the mushrooms through a strainer lined
with a dish towel and reserve the liquid. Leave the
mushrooms whole or slice them, depending on how
large they are. Put the arrowroot in a wok or large pan
and gradually stir in the reserved mushroom liquid.
Add the vegetable stock, sliced ginger, soy sauce, mirin,
rice vinegar, mushrooms, and bok choy and bring to a
boil, stirring constantly. Lower the heat and let simmer
for 15 minutes.

3 Add salt and pepper, but remember that soy sauce is
salty so you might not need any salt at all—taste first.
Use a slotted spoon to remove the pieces of ginger.

4 Divide the noodles among 4 bowls, then spoon the
soup over and garnish with chives.

tomato bruschetta

ingredients

serves 4

8 slices of rustic bread
4 garlic cloves, halved
8 plum tomatoes, peeled
　　and diced
extra virgin olive oil,
　　for drizzling
salt and pepper
fresh basil leaves, to garnish

method

1　Preheat the broiler. Lightly toast the bread on both sides. Rub each piece of toast with half a garlic clove and then return to the broiler for a few seconds.

2　Divide the diced tomatoes among the toasts. Season with salt and pepper to taste and drizzle with olive oil. Serve immediately, garnished with basil leaves.

mixed salad selection

ingredients

serves 4–6

1 large egg yolk
1 tbsp Dijon mustard
½ tsp red wine vinegar
5 fl oz/150 ml sunflower oil
salt and pepper
1½ tsp lemon juice
1 tsp salt
1 lb/450 g celery root

carrot salad

1 lb/450 g carrots, peeled
2 tbsp olive oil
2 tbsp freshly squeezed
    orange juice
salt and pepper
2 tbsp finely chopped almonds
1 tbsp finely chopped fresh
    flat-leaf parsley

beet salad

14 oz/400 g cooked beet, peeled
2 tbsp vinaigrette
1 tbsp snipped fresh chives
slices of French bread and unsalted
    butter, to serve

method

1 To make the rémoulade sauce, whiz the egg yolk, mustard, and red wine vinegar in a food processor or blender until blended. With the motor still running, pour the oil through the feed tube, drop by drop, until the sauce starts to thicken, then add the remainder of the oil in a slow, steady stream. Season with salt and pepper.

2 Put the lemon juice and salt in a large bowl of water. Finely shred the celery root into the acidulated water to prevent discoloration. Drain and pat dry, then stir into the rémoulade sauce. Let stand for 20 minutes at room temperature before serving.

3 To make the carrot salad, finely shred the carrots into a bowl with the olive oil and orange juice and toss together. Season with salt and pepper and cover and chill until required. Stir in the almonds and parsley just before serving.

4 To make the beet salad, cut the beet into ¼-inch/5-mm dice. Put the diced beet in a bowl, then add the vinaigrette and toss together. Cover and chill until required. Stir in the chives just before serving.

5 To serve, divide the celery root rémoulade, carrot salad, and beet salad among individual plates and accompany with plenty of French bread and butter.

figs with blue cheese

ingredients

serves 6

100 g/3½ oz/½ cup superfine sugar
4 oz/115 g/generous ¾ cup whole
  almonds, blanched or
  unblanched
12 ripe figs
12 oz/350 g Spanish blue cheese,
  such as Picós, crumbled
extra virgin olive oil

method

1 First make the caramelized almonds. Put the sugar in a pan over medium-high heat and stir until the sugar melts, turns golden brown, and bubbles: do not stir once the mixture starts to bubble.

2 Remove from the heat and add the almonds one at a time and quickly turn with a fork until coated; if the caramel hardens, return the pan to the heat. Transfer each almond to a lightly buttered cookie sheet once it is coated. Let stand until cool and firm.

3 To serve, slice the figs in half and arrange 4 halves on each plate. Coarsely chop the almonds by hand, reserving a few whole ones for garnish. Place a mound of blue cheese on each plate and sprinkle with chopped almonds. Drizzle the figs very lightly with the oil and garnish with the reserved, whole almonds.

variation

Try replacing the figs with pears for a tasty alternative.

sautéed garlic mushrooms

ingredients

serves 6

1 lb/450 g white mushrooms
5 tbsp Spanish olive oil
2 garlic cloves, finely chopped
squeeze of lemon juice
salt and pepper
4 tbsp chopped fresh
    flat-leaf parsley
crusty bread, to serve

method

1 Wipe or brush clean the mushrooms, then trim off the stalks close to the caps. Cut any large mushrooms in half or into fourths. Heat the olive oil in a large, heavy-bottom skillet, add the garlic and cook for 30 seconds–1 minute, or until lightly browned. Add the mushrooms and sauté over high heat, stirring most of the time, until the mushrooms have absorbed all the oil in the skillet.

2 Reduce the heat to low. When the juices have come out of the mushrooms, increase the heat again, and sauté for 4–5 minutes, stirring most of the time, until the juices have almost evaporated. Add a squeeze of lemon juice and season with salt and pepper. Stir in the chopped parsley and cook for an additional minute.

3 Transfer the sautéed mushrooms to a warmed serving dish and serve piping hot or warm. Accompany with chunks or slices of crusty bread for mopping up the garlic cooking juices.

zucchini fritters with yogurt dip

ingredients

serves 4

2–3 zucchini, about 14 oz/400 g
1 garlic clove, crushed
3 scallions, finely sliced
4½ oz/125 g Feta cheese, crumbled
2 tbsp finely chopped
    fresh parsley
2 tbsp finely chopped
    fresh mint
1 tbsp finely chopped fresh dill
½ tsp freshly grated nutmeg
2 tbsp all-purpose flour
pepper
2 eggs
2 tbsp olive oil
1 lemon, cut into fourths,
    to garnish

yogurt dip

9 oz/250 g/scant 1¼ cups strained
    plain yogurt
¼ cucumber, diced
1 tbsp finely chopped fresh dill
pepper

method

1 Grate the zucchini straight onto a clean dish towel and cover with another. Pat well and let stand for 10 minutes until the zucchini are dry.

2 Meanwhile, to make the dip, mix the yogurt, cucumber, dill, and pepper in a serving bowl. Cover and let chill.

3 Tip the zucchini into a large bowl. Stir in the garlic, scallions, cheese, herbs, nutmeg, flour, and pepper. Beat the eggs in a separate bowl and stir into the zucchini mixture—the batter will be quite lumpy and uneven but this is fine.

4 Heat the oil in a large, wide pan over medium heat. Drop 4 tablespoonfuls of the batter into the skillet, with space in between, and cook for 2–3 minutes on each side. Remove, drain on paper towels, and keep warm. Cook the second batch of fritters in the same way. (There should be 8 fritters in total.)

5 Serve the fritters hot with the dip, garnished with lemon fourths.

stuffed eggplant slices

ingredients

serves 4

1 medium eggplant
4 tbsp extra virgin olive oil
4 oz/115 g/1 cup grated
 mozzarella cheese
1 tbsp fresh chopped basil
14 oz/400 g canned, chopped
 tomatoes with added herbs
extra basil leaves, to garnish

method

1 Slice the eggplant lengthwise into 8 slices. Brush the slices with oil and place on a baking sheet. Bake in a preheated oven, 400°F/200°C for 10 minutes, without letting them get too floppy. Remove from the oven. Sprinkle the grated cheese and basil over the eggplant slices.

2 Roll up each slice and place the slices in a single layer in a shallow ovenproof dish. Pour the chopped tomatoes over them and cook in the oven for 10 minutes or until the sauce bubbles and the cheese melts.

3 Remove the stuffed eggplant slices from the oven and transfer carefully to serving plates. Spoon any remaining chopped tomatoes on or around the eggplant slices. Garnish with basil leaves and serve while still hot.

asparagus with melted butter

ingredients

serves 2

16–20 stalks of asparagus,
   trimmed to about
   8 inches/20 cm
3 oz/85 g unsalted butter, melted
sea salt and pepper, to serve

method

1 Remove some of the base of the asparagus stalks with a potato peeler if they are rather thick. Tie the stalks together with string or use a wire basket so that they can easily be removed from the pan without damage.

2 Bring a large pan of salted water to a boil and plunge in the stalks. Cover with a lid and cook for 4–5 minutes. Pierce one stalk near the base with a sharp knife. If it is fairly soft remove from the heat at once. Do not overcook asparagus or the tender tips will fall off.

3 Drain the asparagus thoroughly and serve on large warmed plates with the butter poured over. Both the butter and the asparagus should be warm rather than hot. Serve with sea salt and pepper for sprinkling.

vegetable tartlets

ingredients

makes 12 tartlets

butter, for greasing
12 ready-baked pastry shells
2 tbsp olive oil
1 red bell pepper, seeded and diced
1 garlic clove, crushed
1 small onion, finely chopped
8 oz/225 g ripe tomatoes, chopped
1 tbsp torn fresh basil
1 tsp fresh or dried thyme
salt and pepper
green salad, to serve

method

1 Grease several baking sheets.

2 Place the ready-baked pastry shells on the prepared baking sheets.

3 Heat the oil in a skillet, add the bell pepper, garlic, and onion, and cook over high heat for about 3 minutes until soft.

4 Add the tomatoes, herbs, and seasoning and spoon onto the pastry shells.

5 Bake in a preheated oven, 400°F/200°C, for about 5 minutes, or until the filling is piping hot. Serve warm with a green salad.

cheese & herb soufflés with sautéed mushrooms

ingredients

makes 6

2 oz/55 g butter, plus extra,
    melted, for greasing
1¹⁄₂ oz/40 g/¹⁄₃ cup
    all-purpose flour
5 fl oz/150 ml/²⁄₃ cup milk
9 oz/250 g/generous 1 cup
    ricotta cheese
4 eggs, separated, plus 2 egg
    whites
2 tbsp finely chopped fresh parsley
2 tbsp finely chopped fresh thyme
1 tbsp finely chopped fresh
    rosemary
salt and pepper
7 fl oz/200 ml/scant 1 cup
    light cream
6 tbsp grated Parmesan cheese
sautéed white mushrooms,
    to serve

method

1 Brush 6 x 3¹⁄₂-inch/9-cm soufflé dishes well with melted butter and set aside. Melt the butter in a medium pan, add the flour, and cook for 30 seconds, stirring constantly. Whisk in the milk and continue whisking over low heat until the mixture thickens. Cook for 30 seconds. Remove from the heat and beat in the ricotta. Add the egg yolks and herbs and season well with salt and pepper.

2 Beat the egg whites in a clean bowl until they form stiff peaks and gently fold them through the ricotta mixture. Spoon into the prepared dishes, filling them just to the top. Place in a baking dish and pour in enough boiling water to come halfway up the sides. Bake the soufflés in a preheated oven, 350°F/180°C, for 15–20 minutes, or until well risen and browned. Remove from the oven, let cool for 10 minutes, then ease out of their molds. Place in a lightly greased ovenproof dish and cover with plastic wrap.

3 Increase the oven temperature to 400°F/200°C. Remove the plastic wrap and pour the cream evenly over the soufflés, sprinkle with Parmesan, and return to the oven for an additional 15 minutes. Serve at once with sautéed mushrooms.

sweet potato, mint & feta patties

ingredients

serves 4

1 lb 5 oz/600 g sweet potatoes, peeled and grated
1 egg, lightly beaten
⅓ cup all-purpose flour
2½ oz/70 g butter, melted
3½ oz/100 g Feta cheese, crumbled
3 tbsp chopped fresh mint
salt and pepper
1 tbsp vegetable oil
4 tbsp sour cream
2 tbsp chopped fresh parsley, to garnish

method

1 Mix the grated sweet potato with the egg, flour, melted butter, Feta, and mint until well combined. Season the mixture with salt and pepper.

2 Heat the oil in a large nonstick skillet over medium heat. Spoon large tablespoons of the mixture into patties, flattening slightly, and cook on both sides in batches until golden.

3 Slide the patties onto a cookie sheet covered with parchment paper and bake in a preheated oven, 325°F/160°C, for 15 minutes, or until crisp. Place 2 patties on each plate, top with a tablespoon of sour cream, and garnish with a little chopped parsley. Serve at once.

beans, nuts & tofu

tuscan bean stew

ingredients

serves 4

1 large fennel bulb
2 tbsp olive oil
1 red onion, cut into small wedges
2–4 garlic cloves, sliced
1 fresh green chile, seeded
    and chopped
1 small eggplant, about
    8 oz/225 g, cut into chunks
2 tbsp tomato paste
16 fl oz–1 pint/450–600 ml/scant
    2–2½ cups vegetable stock
1 lb/450 g ripe tomatoes
1 tbsp balsamic vinegar
a few sprigs of fresh oregano
14 oz/400 g canned cranberry
    beans
14 oz/400 g canned flageolets
1 yellow bell pepper, seeded
    and cut into small strips
1 zucchini, sliced into half moons
55 g/2 oz/⅓ cup pitted black olives
salt and pepper
25 g/1 oz Parmesan cheese,
    freshly shaved
polenta wedges or crusty bread,
    to serve

method

1 Trim the fennel and reserve any feathery fronds, then cut the bulb into small strips. Heat the oil in a large, heavy-bottom pan with a tight-fitting lid, and cook the onion, garlic, chile, and fennel strips, stirring frequently, for 5–8 minutes, or until softened.

2 Add the eggplant and cook, stirring frequently, for 5 minutes. Blend the tomato paste with a little of the stock in a pitcher and pour over the fennel mixture, then add the remaining stock, and the tomatoes, vinegar, and oregano. Bring to a boil, then reduce the heat and simmer, covered, for 15 minutes, or until the tomatoes have begun to collapse.

3 Drain and rinse the beans, then drain again. Add them to the pan with the yellow bell pepper, zucchini, and olives. Simmer for an additional 15 minutes, or until the vegetables are tender. Taste and adjust the seasoning. Scatter with the Parmesan shavings and serve garnished with the reserved fennel fronds, accompanied by polenta wedges or crusty bread.

kidney bean risotto

ingredients

serves 4

4 tbsp olive oil
1 onion, chopped
2 garlic cloves, finely chopped
6 oz/175 g/generous ¾ cup
    brown rice
20 fl oz/625 ml/2½ cups
    vegetable stock
salt and pepper
1 red bell pepper, seeded
    and chopped
2 celery stalks, sliced
8 oz/225 g cremini mushrooms,
    thinly sliced
15 oz/425 g canned red kidney
    beans, drained and rinsed
3 tbsp chopped fresh parsley,
    plus extra to garnish
2 oz/55 g/scant ⅜ cup cashews

method

1 Heat half the oil in a large, heavy-bottom pan. Add the onion and cook, stirring occasionally, for 5 minutes, or until softened. Add half the garlic and cook, stirring frequently, for 2 minutes, then add the rice and stir for 1 minute, or until the grains are thoroughly coated with the oil.

2 Add the stock and a pinch of salt and bring to a boil, stirring constantly. Reduce the heat, cover, and let simmer for 35–40 minutes, or until all the liquid has been absorbed.

3 Meanwhile, heat the remaining oil in a heavy-bottom skillet. Add the bell pepper and celery and cook, stirring frequently, for 5 minutes. Add the sliced mushrooms and the remaining garlic and cook, stirring frequently, for 4–5 minutes.

4 Stir the rice into the skillet. Add the beans, parsley, and cashews. Season with salt and pepper and cook, stirring constantly, until hot. Transfer to a warmed serving dish, sprinkle with extra parsley, and serve at once.

lentil bolognese

ingredients

serves 4

1 tsp vegetable oil
1 tsp minced garlic
1 oz/25 g onion, finely chopped
1 oz/25 g leek, finely chopped
1 oz/25 g celery, finely chopped
1 oz/25 g green bell pepper,
    seeded and finely chopped
1 oz/25 g carrot, finely chopped
1 oz/25 g zucchini, finely chopped
3 oz/85 g flat mushrooms, diced
4 tbsp red wine
pinch of dried thyme
14 oz/400 g canned tomatoes,
    chopped, strained through
    a colander, and the juice and
    pulp reserved separately
4 tbsp dried Puy or green lentils,
    cooked
pepper, to taste
2 tsp lemon juice
1 tsp sugar
3 tbsp chopped fresh basil, plus
    extra sprigs to garnish
freshly cooked spaghetti, to serve

method

1 Heat a pan over a low heat, add the oil and garlic and cook, stirring, until golden brown. Add all the vegetables, except the mushrooms, increase the heat to medium and cook, stirring occasionally, for 10–12 minutes, or until softened and there is no liquid from the vegetables left in the pan. Add the mushrooms.

2 Increase the heat to high, add the wine, and cook for 2 minutes. Add the thyme and the juice from the tomatoes and cook until reduced by half.

3 Add the lentils and pepper, stir in the tomatoes, and cook for a further 3–4 minutes. Remove the pan from the heat and stir in the lemon juice, sugar, and basil.

4 Serve the sauce with freshly cooked spaghetti, garnished with basil sprigs.

variation

Add some kidney beans and chile flakes and serve with rice to turn this into a lentil and bean chili.

spiced lentils with spinach

ingredients

serves 4–6

2 tbsp olive oil
1 large onion, finely chopped
1 large garlic clove, crushed
½ tbsp ground cumin
½ tsp ground ginger
9 oz/250 g/generous 1 cup
    Puy lentils
generous 1 pint/600 ml/2½ cups
    vegetable stock
4 oz/115 g young spinach leaves
2 tbsp fresh mint leaves
1 tbsp fresh cilantro leaves
1 tbsp fresh flat-leaf parsley leaves
freshly squeezed lemon juice
salt and pepper
strips of lemon zest, to garnish

method

1 Heat the oil in a large skillet over medium heat. Add the onion and cook, stirring occasionally, for about 6 minutes. Stir in the garlic, cumin, and ginger and cook, stirring occasionally, until the onion starts to brown.

2 Stir in the lentils. Pour in enough stock to cover the lentils by 1 inch/2.5 cm and bring to a boil. Lower the heat and simmer for 20–30 minutes until the lentils are tender.

3 Meanwhile, rinse the spinach leaves in several changes of cold water and shake dry. Finely chop the mint, cilantro leaves, and parsley.

4 If there isn't any stock left in the pan, add a little extra. Add the spinach and stir through until it just wilts. Stir in the mint, cilantro, and parsley. Adjust the seasoning, adding lemon juice and salt and pepper. Transfer to a serving bowl and serve, garnished with lemon zest.

warm red lentil salad with goat cheese

ingredients

serves 4

2 tbsp olive oil
2 tsp cumin seeds
2 garlic cloves, crushed
2 tsp grated fresh ginger
10½ oz/300 g/1½ cups
    red lentils
24 fl oz/750 ml/3 cups
    vegetable stock
2 tbsp chopped fresh mint
2 tbsp chopped fresh cilantro
2 red onions, thinly sliced
7 oz/200 g baby spinach leaves
1 tsp hazelnut oil
5½ oz/150 g soft goat cheese
4 tbsp strained plain yogurt
pepper
1 lemon, cut into fourths,
    to garnish
toasted rye bread, to serve

method

1 Heat half the olive oil in a large pan over medium heat, add the cumin seeds, garlic, and ginger, and cook for 2 minutes, stirring constantly.

2 Stir in the lentils, then add the stock, a ladleful at a time, until it is all absorbed, stirring constantly—this will take about 20 minutes. Remove from the heat and stir in the herbs.

3 Meanwhile, heat the remaining olive oil in a skillet over medium heat, add the onions, and cook, stirring frequently, for 10 minutes, or until soft and lightly browned.

4 Toss the spinach in the hazelnut oil in a bowl, then divide among 4 serving plates.

5 Mash the goat cheese with the yogurt in a small bowl and season with pepper.

6 Divide the lentils among the serving plates and top with the onions and goat cheese mixture. Garnish with lemon fourths and serve with toasted rye bread.

mixed vegetable curry with chickpea pancakes

ingredients

serves 4

7 oz/200 g carrots
10½ oz/300 g potatoes
2 tbsp vegetable oil
1½ tsp cumin seeds
seeds from 5 cardamom pods
1½ tsp mustard seeds
2 onions, grated
1 tsp ground turmeric
1 tsp ground coriander
1½ tsp chili powder
1 tbsp grated fresh ginger
2 large garlic cloves, crushed
9 fl oz/250 ml/scant 1¼ cups
    strained tomatoes
7 fl oz/200 ml/scant 1 cup
    vegetable stock
4 oz/115 g/1 cup frozen peas
4 oz/115 g frozen spinach leaves

chickpea pancakes

8 oz/225 g/generous
    1½ cups chickpea flour
½ tsp baking soda
14 fl oz/400 ml/1¾ cups water
vegetable oil, for cooking

method

1 To make the pancakes, sift the flour, and baking soda into a large mixing bowl. Make a well in the center and add the water. Using a balloon whisk, gradually mix the flour into the water to form a smooth batter. Add salt if preferred. Let stand for 15 minutes.

2 Heat enough oil to cover the bottom of a skillet over medium heat. Add a small quantity of batter to the skillet, and cook for 3 minutes on each side until golden. Repeat with the remaining batter to make 8 pancakes.

3 Meanwhile, cut the carrots into chunks and the potatoes into fourths. Place in a steamer and steam until just tender.

4 Heat the oil in a large pan over medium heat and fry the cumin, cardamom, and mustard seeds until they start to sizzle. Add the onions, partially cover, and cook over medium-low heat, until soft and golden.

5 Add the other spices, ginger, and garlic and cook, stirring, for 1 minute. Add the strained tomatoes, stock, carrots, and potatoes, partially cover, and cook for 10–15 minutes, or until the vegetables are tender. Add the peas and spinach, then cook for 2–3 minutes. Serve with the warm pancakes.

baby corn with dal

ingredients

serves 4

8 oz/225 g/generous 1 cup
    red lentils
2 tbsp vegetable oil
1 tsp cumin seeds
1 tsp ground coriander
½ tsp asafetida
1 fresh red chile, seeded and
    finely chopped
4 oz/115 g green beans, chopped,
    blanched, and drained
1 green bell pepper, seeded
    and chopped
4 oz/115 g baby corn, sliced
    diagonally
5 fl oz/150 ml/⅔ cup
    vegetable stock
2 tomatoes, seeded and chopped
1 tbsp chopped fresh cilantro
1 tbsp poppy seeds

method

1 Rinse the lentils 2–3 times in cold water. Put into a large pan and cover with cold water. Bring to a boil, then reduce the heat and let simmer for 15–20 minutes, or until tender. Drain, return to the pan, and keep warm.

2 Meanwhile, heat the oil in a separate pan over low heat, add the spices and chile, and cook for 2 minutes, stirring constantly. Add the green beans, green bell pepper, and baby corn and cook for 2 minutes, stirring constantly.

3 Stir in the stock and bring to a boil, then reduce the heat and let simmer for 5 minutes, or until the vegetables are just tender.

4 Stir the vegetables and their liquid into the cooked lentils with the tomatoes and heat through for 5–8 minutes, or until piping hot.

5 Serve the dish at once sprinkled with the cilantro and poppy seeds.

bean burgers

ingredients

serves 4

1 tbsp sunflower oil, plus
    extra for brushing
1 onion, finely chopped
1 garlic clove, finely chopped
1 tsp ground coriander
1 tsp ground cumin
4 oz/115 g white mushrooms,
    finely chopped
15 oz/425 g canned pinto or
    red kidney beans, drained
    and rinsed
2 tbsp chopped fresh flat-leaf
    parsley
salt and pepper
all-purpose flour, for dusting
hamburger buns
salad, to serve

method

1 Heat the oil in a heavy-bottom skillet over medium heat. Add the onion and cook, stirring frequently, for 5 minutes, or until softened. Add the garlic, coriander, and cumin and cook, stirring, for an additional minute. Add the mushrooms and cook, stirring frequently, for 4–5 minutes until all the liquid has evaporated. Transfer to a bowl.

2 Put the beans in a small bowl and mash with a fork. Stir into the mushroom mixture with the parsley and season with salt and pepper.

3 Preheat the broiler to medium-high. Divide the mixture equally into 4 portions, dust lightly with flour, and shape into flat, round patties. Brush with oil and cook under the broiler for 4–5 minutes on each side. Serve in hamburger buns with salad.

chili bean cakes with avocado salsa

ingredients

serves 4

2 oz/55 g/³/₈ cup pine nuts
15 oz/425 g canned mixed beans
½ red onion, finely chopped
1 tbsp tomato paste
½ fresh red chile, seeded and
    finely chopped
2 oz/55 g/1 cup fresh brown
    bread crumbs
1 egg, beaten
1 tbsp finely chopped fresh cilantro
2 tbsp corn oil
1 lime, cut into fourths, to garnish
4 toasted whole-wheat bread rolls,
    to serve (optional)

salsa

1 avocado, pitted, peeled,
    and chopped
3½ oz/100 g tomatoes, seeded
    and chopped
2 garlic cloves, crushed
2 tbsp finely chopped fresh cilantro
1 tbsp olive oil
pepper
juice of ½ lime

method

1 Heat a nonstick skillet over medium heat, add the pine nuts, and cook, turning, until just browned. Tip into a bowl and set aside.

2 Put the drained beans into a large bowl and coarsely mash. Add the onion, tomato paste, chile, pine nuts, and half the bread crumbs and mix well. Add half the egg and the cilantro and mash together, adding a little more egg, if needed, to bind the mixture. Form the mixture into 4 flat cakes. Coat with the remaining bread crumbs, cover, and let chill in the refrigerator for 30 minutes.

3 To make the salsa, mix all the ingredients together in a serving bowl, cover, and let chill in the refrigerator until required.

4 Heat the oil in a skillet over medium heat, add the bean cakes, and cook for 4–5 minutes on each side, or until crisp and heated through. Remove from the skillet and drain on paper towels.

5 Serve each bean cake in a toasted whole-wheat roll, if desired, with the salsa, garnished with a lime fourth.

toasted pine nut & vegetable couscous

ingredients

serves 4

4 oz/115 g/generous ½ cup
  dried green lentils
2 oz/55 g/⅜ cup pine nuts
1 tbsp olive oil
1 onion, diced
2 garlic cloves, crushed
10 oz/280 g zucchini, sliced
9 oz/250 g tomatoes, chopped
14 oz/400 g canned artichoke
  hearts, drained and cut in
  half lengthwise
9 oz/250 g/generous
  1¼ cups couscous
16 fl oz/500 ml/2 cups
  vegetable stock
3 tbsp torn fresh basil leaves,
  plus extra leaves to garnish
pepper

method

1 Put the lentils into a pan with plenty of cold water, bring to a boil, and boil rapidly for 10 minutes. Reduce the heat, cover, and let simmer until tender.

2 Meanwhile, preheat the broiler to medium. Spread the pine nuts out in a single layer on a cookie sheet and toast under the preheated broiler, turning to brown evenly—watch constantly because they brown very quickly. Tip the pine nuts into a small dish and set aside.

3 Heat the oil in a skillet over medium heat, add the onion, garlic, and zucchini and cook, stirring frequently, for 8–10 minutes, or until tender and the zucchini have browned slightly. Add the tomatoes and artichoke halves and heat through thoroughly for 5 minutes.

4 Meanwhile, put the couscous into a heatproof bowl. Bring the stock to a boil in a pan and pour over the couscous, cover, and let stand for 10 minutes until the couscous absorbs the stock and becomes tender.

5 Drain the lentils and stir into the couscous. Stir in the torn basil leaves and season well with pepper. Transfer to a warmed serving dish and spoon over the cooked vegetables. Sprinkle the pine nuts over the top, garnish with basil leaves, and serve at once.

falafel burgers

ingredients

serves 4

2 x 14 oz/400 g can chickpeas,
    drained and rinsed
1 small onion, chopped
zest and juice of 1 lime
2 tsp ground coriander
2 tsp ground cumin
6 tbsp all-purpose flour
4 tbsp olive oil
4 fresh basil sprigs, to garnish
tomato salsa, to serve

method

1 Put the chickpeas, onion, lime zest and juice, and the
   spices into a food processor and process to a coarse paste.

2 Tip the mixture out onto a clean counter or cutting
   board and shape into 4 patties.

3 Spread the flour out on a large flat plate and use to
   coat the patties.

4 Heat the oil in a large skillet, add the burgers, and cook
   for 2 minutes on each side until crisp. Garnish with
   basil and serve with tomato salsa.

wilted spinach, yogurt & walnut salad

ingredients

serves 2

1 lb/450 g fresh spinach leaves
1 onion, chopped
1 tbsp olive oil
8 fl oz/225 ml/1 cup plain yogurt
1 garlic clove, finely chopped
2 tbsp chopped toasted walnuts
2–3 tsp chopped fresh mint
salt and pepper
pita bread, to serve

method

1 Put the spinach and onion into a pan, cover, and cook gently for a few minutes until the spinach has wilted.

2 Add the oil and cook for an additional 5 minutes. Season with salt and pepper to taste.

3 Combine the yogurt and garlic in a bowl.

4 Put the spinach and onion into a serving bowl and pour over the yogurt mixture. Scatter over the walnuts and chopped mint and serve with pita bread.

celery root, chestnut, spinach & feta filo pies

ingredients

serves 4

4 tbsp olive oil

2 garlic cloves, crushed

½ large or 1 whole small head celery root, cut into short thin sticks

9 oz/250 g baby spinach leaves

3 oz/85 g/scant ½ cup cooked, peeled chestnuts, coarsely chopped

7 oz/200 g Feta cheese (drained weight), crumbled

1 egg

2 tbsp pesto sauce

1 tbsp finely chopped fresh parsley

pepper

4 sheets filo pastry, about 13 x 7 inches/ 32 x 18 cm each

method

1 Heat 1 tablespoon of the oil in a large skillet over medium heat, add the garlic, and cook for 1 minute, stirring constantly. Add the celery root and cook for 5 minutes, or until soft and browned. Remove from the skillet and keep warm.

2 Add 1 tablespoon of the remaining oil to the skillet, then add the spinach, cover, and cook for 2–3 minutes, or until the spinach has wilted. Uncover and cook until any liquid has evaporated.

3 Mix the garlic and celery root, spinach, chestnuts, cheese, egg, pesto, parsley, and pepper in a large bowl. Divide the mixture among 4 individual gratin dishes or put it all into 1 medium gratin dish.

4 Brush each sheet of filo with the remaining oil and arrange, slightly scrunched, on top of the celery root mixture and bake in a preheated oven, 375°F/190°C, for 15–20 minutes, or until browned. Serve at once.

nutty blue cheese roast

ingredients

serves 6–8

2 tbsp virgin olive oil,
   plus extra for oiling
2 onions, one finely chopped and
   one cut into thin wedges
3–5 garlic cloves, crushed
2 celery stalks, finely sliced
6 oz/175 g/scant 1 cup cooked
   and peeled chestnuts
6 oz/175 g/generous 1 cup
   mixed chopped nuts
2 oz/55 g/generous ½ cup
   ground almonds
2 oz/55 g/1 cup fresh whole
   wheat bread crumbs
8 oz/225 g blue cheese, crumbled
1 tbsp chopped fresh basil, plus
   extra sprigs to garnish
1 egg, beaten
salt and pepper
1 red bell pepper, peeled, seeded,
   and cut into thin wedges
1 zucchini, about 4 oz/115 g,
   cut into wedges
cherry tomatoes, to garnish
tomato ketchup, to serve

method

1 Heat 1 tablespoon of the oil in a skillet over medium heat, add the chopped onion, 1–2 of the garlic cloves, and the celery and cook for 5 minutes, stirring occasionally.

2 Remove from the skillet, drain through a strainer and transfer to a food processor with the nuts, bread crumbs, half the cheese, and the basil. Using the pulse button, blend the ingredients together, then slowly blend in the egg to form a stiff mixture. Season.

3 Heat the remaining oil in a skillet over medium heat, add the onion wedges, remaining garlic, red bell pepper, and zucchini and cook for 5 minutes, stirring frequently. Remove from the skillet, add salt and pepper, and drain through a strainer.

4 Place half the nut mixture in a lightly oiled 2-lb/900-g loaf pan and smooth the surface. Cover with the onion and bell pepper mixture and crumble over the remaining cheese. Top with the remaining nut mixture and press down firmly. Cover with foil. Bake in a preheated oven, 350°F/180°C, for 45 minutes. Remove the foil and bake for 25–35 minutes, until firm.

5 Remove from the oven, let cool in the pan for 5 minutes, then turn out and serve in slices garnished with basil sprigs, cherry tomatoes, and a little tomato ketchup.

vegetable & hazelnut loaf

ingredients

serves 4

2 tbsp sunflower oil, plus extra
   for oiling
1 onion, chopped
1 garlic clove, finely chopped
2 celery stalks, chopped
1 tbsp all-purpose flour
7 fl oz/200 ml/scant 1 cup
   strained canned tomatoes
4 oz/115 g/2 cups fresh
   whole-wheat bread crumbs
2 carrots, grated
4 oz/115 g/³/₄ cup toasted
   hazelnuts, ground
1 tbsp dark soy sauce
2 tbsp chopped fresh cilantro
1 egg, lightly beaten
salt and pepper
mixed red and green lettuce
   leaves, to serve

method

1 Oil and line a 1-lb/450-g loaf pan. Heat the oil in a heavy-bottom skillet over medium heat. Add the onion and cook, stirring frequently, for 5 minutes, or until softened. Add the garlic and celery and cook, stirring frequently, for 5 minutes. Add the flour and cook, stirring constantly, for 1 minute. Gradually stir in the strained canned tomatoes and cook, stirring constantly, until thickened. Remove the skillet from the heat.

2 Put the bread crumbs, carrots, ground hazelnuts, soy sauce, and cilantro in a bowl. Add the tomato mixture and stir well. Let cool slightly, then beat in the egg and season with salt and pepper.

3 Spoon the mixture into the prepared pan and smooth the surface. Cover with foil and bake in a preheated oven, 350°F/180°C for 1 hour. If serving hot, turn the loaf out on to a warmed serving dish and serve immediately with mixed red and green salad leaves. Alternatively, let the loaf cool in the pan before turning out.

tofu stir-fry

ingredients

serves 4

2 tbsp sunflower or olive oil
12 oz/350 g firm tofu, cubed
8 oz/225 g bok choy, coarsely
    chopped
1 garlic clove, chopped
4 tbsp sweet chili sauce
2 tbsp light soy sauce

method

1 Heat 1 tablespoon of oil in a wok, add the tofu in batches, and stir-fry for 2–3 minutes until golden. Remove and set aside.

2 Add the bok choy to the wok and stir-fry for a few seconds until tender and wilted. Remove and set aside.

3 Add the remaining oil to the wok, then add the garlic and stir-fry for 30 seconds.

4 Stir in the chili sauce and soy sauce and bring to a boil.

5 Return the tofu and bok choy to the wok and toss gently until coated in the sauce. Serve immediately.

thai bean curd cakes with chili dip

ingredients

serves 4

10½ oz/300 g firm bean curd,
    drained weight, coarsely grated
1 lemongrass stalk, outer layer
    discarded, finely chopped
2 garlic cloves, chopped
1-inch/2.5-cm piece fresh
    ginger, grated
2 kaffir lime leaves, finely chopped
2 shallots, finely chopped
2 fresh red chiles, seeded and
    finely chopped
4 tbsp chopped fresh cilantro
3¼ oz/90 g/scant ¾ cup
    gluten-free all-purpose flour
½ tsp salt
corn oil, for cooking

chili dip

3 tbsp white distilled vinegar
    or rice wine vinegar
2 scallions, finely sliced
1 tbsp superfine sugar
2 fresh chiles, finely chopped
2 tbsp chopped fresh cilantro
pinch of salt

method

1 To make the chili dip, mix all the ingredients together
in a small serving bowl and set aside.

2 Mix the bean curd with the lemongrass, garlic, ginger,
lime leaves, if using, shallots, chiles, and cilantro in a
mixing bowl. Stir in the flour and salt to make a coarse,
sticky paste. Cover and let chill in the refrigerator for
1 hour to let the mixture firm up slightly.

3 Form the mixture into 8 large walnut-size balls and,
using floured hands, flatten into circles. Heat enough
oil to cover the bottom of a large, heavy-bottom skillet
over medium heat. Cook the cakes in 2 batches,
turning halfway through, for 4–6 minutes, or until
golden brown. Drain on paper towels and serve warm
with the chili dip.

pasta, noodles & rice

pasta with olive sauce

ingredients

serves 2–4

12 oz/350 g fresh pasta shapes
6 tbsp olive oil
½ tsp freshly grated nutmeg
½ tsp black pepper
1 garlic clove, crushed
2 tbsp tapenade
3 oz/85 g/½ cup black or green
    olives, pitted and sliced
1 tbsp chopped fresh parsley,
    to garnish (optional)
salt

method

1 Cook the pasta in a large pan of boiling salted water for about 4 minutes, or according to the package directions until tender but still firm to the bite.

2 Meanwhile, put ½ teaspoon of salt with the oil, nutmeg, pepper, garlic, tapenade, and olives in another pan and heat slowly but do not allow to boil. Cover and let stand for 3–4 minutes.

3 Drain the pasta and return to the pan. Add the olives in the flavored oil and heat gently for 1–2 minutes. Serve immediately, garnished with chopped parsley, if using.

macaroni & cheese

ingredients

serves 4

8 oz/225 g macaroni
1 egg, beaten
4½ oz/125 g/1¼ cups sharp
    Cheddar cheese, grated
1 tbsp wholegrain mustard
2 tbsp chopped fresh chives
20 fl oz/625 ml/2½ cups
    béchamel sauce
salt and pepper
4 tomatoes, sliced
4½ oz/125 g/1¼ cups Red Leicester
    cheese, grated
2¼ oz/60 g/generous ½ cup blue
    cheese, grated
2 tbsp sunflower seeds
snipped fresh chives, to garnish

béchamel sauce

20 fl oz/600 ml/2½ cups milk
1 bay leaf
6 black peppercorns
slice of onion
mace blade
4 tbsp butter
6 tbsp all-purpose flour
salt and pepper

method

1 To make the béchamel sauce, pour the milk into a pan and add the bay leaf, peppercorns, onion, and mace. Heat to just below boiling point, then remove from the heat, cover, let infuse for 10 minutes, then strain. Melt the butter in a separate pan. Sprinkle in the flour and cook over low heat, stirring constantly, for 1 minute. Gradually stir in the milk, then bring to a boil and cook, stirring, until thickened and smooth. Season.

2 Bring a large pan of lightly salted water to a boil and cook the macaroni for 8–10 minutes, or until just tender. Drain well and place in an ovenproof dish.

3 Stir the beaten egg, Cheddar cheese, mustard, and chives into the béchamel sauce and season with salt and pepper. Spoon the mixture over the macaroni, making sure it is well covered. Top with a layer of the sliced tomatoes.

4 Sprinkle the Red Leicester cheese, blue cheese, and sunflower seeds over the top. Place on a cookie sheet and bake in a preheated oven, 375°F/190°C, for 25–30 minutes, or until bubbling and golden. Garnish with snipped fresh chives and serve at once.

vegetarian lasagna

ingredients

serves 4

olive oil, for brushing
2 eggplants, sliced
2 tbsp butter
1 garlic clove, finely chopped
4 zucchini, sliced
1 tbsp finely chopped fresh
    flat-leaf parsley and marjoram
8 oz/225 g mozzarella cheese,
    grated
20 fl oz/625 ml/2½ cups strained
    canned tomatoes
175 g/6 oz dried no-precook
    lasagna
salt and pepper
béchamel sauce (see below)
2 oz/55 g/½ cup freshly grated
    Parmesan cheese

béchamel sauce
10 fl oz/300 ml/1¼ cups milk
1 bay leaf
6 black peppercorns
slice of onion
mace blade
2 tbsp butter
3 tbsp all-purpose flour
salt and pepper

method

1 To make the béchamel sauce, pour the milk into a pan and add the bay leaf, peppercorns, onion, and mace. Heat to just below boiling point, then remove from the heat, cover, let infuse for 10 minutes, then strain. Melt the butter in a separate pan. Sprinkle in the flour and cook over low heat, stirring constantly, for 1 minute. Gradually stir in the milk, then bring to a boil and cook, stirring, until thickened and smooth. Season.

2 Brush a broiler pan with olive oil and heat until smoking. Add half the eggplant slices and cook over medium heat for 8 minutes, or until golden brown all over. Remove from the broiler pan and drain. Repeat with the remaining eggplant slices.

3 Melt the butter in a skillet and add the garlic, zucchini, parsley, and marjoram. Cook over medium heat, stirring frequently, for 5 minutes, or until the zucchini are golden brown all over. Remove and let drain.

4 Layer the eggplant, zucchini, mozzarella, strained tomatoes, and lasagna in an ovenproof dish brushed with olive oil. Season, and finish with a layer of lasagna. Pour over the béchamel sauce, making sure that all the pasta is covered. Sprinkle with Parmesan cheese and bake in a preheated oven, 400°F/200°C, for 30–40 minutes, or until golden brown. Serve at once.

pasta with pesto

ingredients

serves 4

1 lb/450 g dried tagliatelle
fresh basil sprigs, to garnish

pesto
2 garlic cloves
1 oz/25 g/¼ cup pine nuts
salt
4 oz/115 g fresh basil leaves
2 oz/55 g/½ cup freshly grated
   Parmesan cheese
4 fl oz/125 ml/½ cup olive oil

method

1 To make the pesto, put the garlic, pine nuts, a large pinch of salt, and the basil into a mortar and pound to a paste with a pestle. Transfer to a bowl and gradually work in the Parmesan cheese with a wooden spoon, followed by the olive oil, to make a thick, creamy sauce. Taste and adjust the seasoning if necessary.

2 Alternatively, put the garlic, pine nuts, and a large pinch of salt into a food processor or blender and process briefly. Add the basil leaves and process to a paste. With the motor still running, gradually add the olive oil. Scrape into a bowl and beat in the Parmesan cheese.

3 Bring a large pan of lightly salted water to a boil. Add the pasta, return to a boil, and cook for 8–10 minutes, or until tender but still firm to the bite. Drain the pasta well, return to the pan, and toss with half the pesto, then divide among warmed serving plates and top with the remaining pesto. Garnish with basil sprigs and serve immediately.

creamy spinach & mushroom pasta

ingredients

serves 4

10½ oz/300 g dried
gluten-free penne or
pasta of your choice
2 tbsp olive oil
9 oz/250 g mushrooms, sliced
1 tsp dried oregano
9 fl oz/275 ml/scant 1¼ cups
vegetable stock
1 tbsp lemon juice
6 tbsp cream cheese
7 oz/200 g frozen spinach leaves
salt and pepper

method

1 Cook the pasta in a large pan of lightly salted boiling water, according to the package instructions. Drain, reserving 6 fl oz/175 ml/¾ cup of the cooking liquid.

2 Meanwhile, heat the oil in a large, heavy-bottom skillet over medium heat, add the mushrooms, and cook, stirring frequently, for 8 minutes, or until almost crisp. Stir in the oregano, stock, and lemon juice and cook for 10–12 minutes, or until the sauce is reduced by half.

3 Stir in the cream cheese and spinach and cook over medium-low heat for 3–5 minutes. Add the reserved cooking liquid, then the cooked pasta. Stir well, season with salt and pepper, and heat through gently before serving.

crisp noodle & vegetable stir-fry

ingredients

serves 4

peanut or sunflower oil,
  for deep-frying
4 oz/115 g rice vermicelli,
  broken into 3-inch/7.5-cm
  lengths
4 oz/115 g green beans,
  cut into short lengths
2 carrots, cut into thin sticks
2 zucchini, cut into thin sticks
4 oz/115 g shiitake mushrooms,
  sliced
1-inch/2.5-cm piece fresh ginger,
  shredded
½ small head Napa cabbage,
  shredded
4 scallions, shredded
3 oz/85 g/½ cup bean sprouts
2 tbsp dark soy sauce
2 tbsp Chinese rice wine
large pinch of sugar
2 tbsp coarsely chopped fresh
  cilantro

method

1 Half-fill a wok or deep, heavy-bottom skillet with oil. Heat to 350–375°F/180–190°C, or until a cube of bread browns in 30 seconds.

2 Add the noodles, in batches, and cook for 1½–2 minutes, or until crisp and puffed up. Remove and drain on paper towels. Pour off all but 2 tablespoons of oil from the wok.

3 Heat the remaining oil over high heat. Add the green beans and stir-fry for 2 minutes. Add the carrot and zucchini sticks, sliced mushrooms, and ginger, and stir-fry for 2 minutes.

4 Add the shredded Napa cabbage, scallions, and bean sprouts and stir-fry for an additional 1 minute. Add the soy sauce, rice wine, and sugar and cook, stirring constantly, for 1 minute.

5 Add the chopped cilantro and toss well. Serve immediately, with the noodles.

chinese vegetables & bean sprouts with noodles

ingredients

serves 4

40 fl oz/1.25 liters/5 cups
   vegetable stock
1 garlic clove, crushed
1/2-inch/1-cm piece fresh ginger,
   finely chopped
8 oz/225 g dried medium
   egg noodles
1 red bell pepper, seeded
   and sliced
3 oz/85 g/3/4 cup frozen peas
4 oz/115 g broccoli florets
3 oz/85 g shiitake mushrooms,
   sliced
2 tbsp sesame seeds
8 oz/225 g canned water
   chestnuts, drained and halved
8 oz/225 g canned bamboo shoots,
   drained
10 oz/280 g Napa cabbage, sliced
5 oz/140 g/scant 1 cup
   bean sprouts
3 scallions, sliced
1 tbsp dark soy sauce
pepper

method

1 Bring the stock, garlic, and ginger to a boil in a large
pan. Stir in the noodles, red bell pepper, peas, broccoli,
and mushrooms and return to a boil. Reduce the heat,
cover, and let simmer for 5–6 minutes, or until the
noodles are tender.

2 Meanwhile, preheat the broiler to medium. Spread the
sesame seeds out in a single layer on a cookie sheet
and toast under the preheated broiler, turning to
brown evenly—watch constantly because they brown
very quickly. Tip the sesame seeds into a small dish and
set aside.

3 Once the noodles are tender, add the water chestnuts,
bamboo shoots, Napa cabbage, bean sprouts, and
scallions to the pan. Return the stock to a boil, stir to
mix the ingredients, and let simmer for an additional
2–3 minutes to heat through thoroughly.

4 Carefully drain off 10 fl oz/300 ml/1 1/4 cups of the stock
into a small heatproof pitcher and set aside. Drain and
discard any remaining stock and turn the noodles and
vegetables into a warmed serving dish. Quickly mix
the soy sauce and sesame seeds with the reserved
stock and pour over the dish. Season and serve at once.

sweet-&-sour vegetables on noodle crêpes

ingredients

serves 4

4 oz/115 g dried thin cellophane
    noodles

6 eggs

4 scallions, sliced diagonally

salt and pepper

2½ tbsp peanut or corn oil

2 lb/900 g selection of vegetables,
    such as carrots, baby corn,
    cauliflower, broccoli, snow peas,
    and onions, peeled as necessary
    and chopped into same-size
    pieces

3½ oz/100 g canned bamboo
    shoots, drained

7 oz/200 g/scant 1 cup bottled
    sweet-and-sour sauce

method

1 Soak the noodles in enough lukewarm water to cover
    and let stand for 20 minutes, until soft. Alternatively,
    cook according to the package instructions. Drain them
    well and use scissors to cut into 3-inch/7.5-cm pieces,
    then set aside.

2 Beat the eggs, then stir in the noodles, the scallions,
    salt, and pepper. Heat an 8-inch/20-cm skillet over high
    heat. Add 1 tablespoon oil and swirl it round. Pour in a
    fourth of the egg mixture and tilt the skillet so it covers
    the bottom. Lower the heat to medium and cook for
    1 minute, or until the thin crêpe is set. Flip it over, adding
    a little extra oil, if necessary, and cook the other side
    until golden. Keep warm in a low oven while you make
    3 more crêpes.

3 After you've made 4 crêpes, heat a wok or large,
    heavy-bottom skillet over high heat. Add 1½
    tablespoons oil and heat until it shimmers. Add the
    thickest vegetables, such as carrots, first and stir-fry for
    30 seconds. Gradually add the remaining vegetables
    and bamboo shoots. Stir in the sauce and stir-fry until
    all the vegetables are tender and the sauce is hot.
    Spoon the vegetables and sauce over the crêpes.

wild mushroom risotto

ingredients

serves 6

2 oz/55 g/½ cup dried porcini
or morel mushrooms
4 tbsp olive oil
about 1 lb 2 oz/500 g mixed fresh
wild mushrooms, such as
porcini, horse mushrooms, and
chanterelles, halved if large
3–4 garlic cloves, finely chopped
2 oz/55 g butter
1 onion, finely chopped
12 oz/350 g/1¾ cups Arborio rice
2 fl oz/50 ml/¼ cup dry
white vermouth
40 fl oz/1.25 liters/5 cups
simmering vegetable stock
salt and pepper
4 oz/115 g/1 cup freshly grated
Parmesan cheese
4 tbsp chopped fresh
flat-leaf parsley

method

1 Place the dried mushrooms in a heatproof bowl
and add boiling water to cover. Set aside to soak for
30 minutes, then carefully lift out and pat dry. Strain
the soaking liquid through a strainer lined with paper
towels and set aside.

2 Heat 3 tablespoons of the oil in a large skillet. Add
the fresh mushrooms and stir-fry for 1–2 minutes.
Add the garlic and the soaked mushrooms and cook,
stirring frequently, for 2 minutes. Transfer to a plate.

3 Heat the remaining oil and half the butter in a pan.
Add the onion and cook over medium heat, stirring,
until softened. Reduce the heat, add the rice, and
cook, stirring, until the grains are translucent. Add the
vermouth and cook, stirring, for 1 minute until reduced.

4 Gradually add the hot stock, a ladleful at a time. Stir
constantly and add more liquid as the rice absorbs
each addition. Increase the heat to medium so that
the liquid bubbles. Cook for 20 minutes, or until all the
liquid is absorbed and the rice is creamy.

5 Add half the reserved mushroom soaking liquid
and stir in the mushrooms. Season and add more
mushroom liquid, if necessary. Remove from the heat
and stir in the remaining butter, the grated Parmesan,
and chopped parsley. Serve at once.

risotto primavera

ingredients

serves 6–8

8 oz/225 g fresh thin asparagus
  spears
4 tbsp olive oil
6 oz/175 g young green beans,
  cut into 1-inch/2.5-cm lengths
6 oz/175 g young zucchini,
  quartered and cut into
  1-inch/2.5-cm lengths
8 oz/225 g/generous
  1½ cups shelled fresh peas
1 onion, finely chopped
1–2 garlic cloves, finely
  chopped
12 oz/350 g/1¾ cups
  Arborio rice
52 fl oz/1.6 liters/generous 6⅓
  cups simmering vegetable
  stock
4 scallions, cut into
  1-inch/2.5-cm lengths
salt and pepper
2 oz/55 g butter
4 oz/115 g/1 cup freshly grated
  Parmesan cheese
2 tbsp snipped fresh chives
2 tbsp shredded fresh basil
scallions, to garnish (optional)

method

1 Trim the woody ends of the asparagus and cut off the tips. Cut the stems into 1-inch/2.5-cm pieces and set aside with the tips. Heat 2 tablespoons of the oil in a large skillet over high heat until very hot. Add the asparagus, beans, zucchini, and peas and stir-fry for 3–4 minutes until they are bright green and just starting to soften. Set aside.

2 Heat the remaining oil in a large, heavy-bottom pan over medium heat. Add the onion and cook, stirring occasionally, for 3 minutes, or until it starts to soften. Stir in the garlic and cook, while stirring, for 30 seconds. Reduce the heat, add the rice, and mix to coat in oil. Cook, stirring constantly, for 2–3 minutes, or until the grains are translucent.

3 Add the hot stock, a ladleful at a time. Stir constantly and add more liquid as the rice absorbs each addition. Increase the heat to medium so that the liquid bubbles. Cook for 20 minutes, or until all but 2 tablespoons of the liquid is absorbed and the rice is creamy.

4 Stir in the stir-fried vegetables, and scallions with the remaining stock. Cook for 2 minutes, stirring frequently. Stir in the butter, Parmesan, chives, and basil. Remove the pan from the heat and serve the risotto at once, garnished with scallions, if liked.

spiced risotto cakes

ingredients

serves 3

3 oz/85 g onion, finely chopped
3 oz/85 g leek, finely chopped
1 oz/25g/⅛ cup Arborio rice
18 fl oz/550 ml/scant
      2½ cups vegetable stock
3 oz/85 g/scant ½ cup grated
      zucchini
1 tbsp fresh basil, chopped
1 oz/25g/½ cup fresh whole wheat
      bread crumbs
vegetable oil spray
radicchio leaves, to serve

filling

1¾ oz/50 g/scant ¼ cup cream
      cheese
1¾ oz/50 g mango, diced
1 tsp finely grated lime rind
1 tsp lime juice
pinch of cayenne pepper

method

1 Heat a large, nonstick pan over high heat, add the
onion and leek, and cook, stirring constantly, for
2–3 minutes, or until softened but not colored.

2 Add the rice and stock, bring to a boil, then continue
to boil, stirring constantly, for 2 minutes. Reduce the heat
and cook for an additional 15 minutes, stirring every
2–3 minutes. When the rice is nearly cooked and has
absorbed all the stock, stir in the zucchini and basil and
cook, continuing to stir, over high heat for an additional
5–10 minutes or until the mixture is sticky and dry. Turn
out onto a plate and let cool.

3 Meanwhile, to make the filling, mix the cream cheese,
mango, lime rind and juice, and cayenne together in
a bowl.

4 Divide the cooled rice mixture into 3 and form into
cakes. Make an indentation in the center of each cake
and fill with 1 tbsp of the filling. Mold the sides up and
over to seal in the filling, then reshape with a palette
knife. Coat each cake with bread crumbs and arrange
on a nonstick cookie sheet. Spray each cake lightly
with oil and bake in a preheated oven, 400°F/200°C,
for 15–20 minutes, or until a light golden brown color.
Serve with radicchio leaves.

spicy stuffed bell peppers

ingredients

serves 4

4 assorted colored bell peppers
3 sprays olive oil
1 onion, finely chopped
2 garlic cloves, chopped
1-inch/2.5-cm piece fresh ginger,
    peeled and grated
1–2 fresh serrano chiles, seeded
    and chopped
1 tsp ground cumin
1 tsp ground coriander
3 oz/85 g/scant 1/2 cup cooked
    brown basmati rice
1 large carrot, about 4 oz/115 g,
    peeled and grated
1 large zucchini, about
    3 oz/85 g, trimmed and grated
1 oz/25 g/scant 1/4 cup plumped
    dried apricots, finely chopped
1 tbsp chopped fresh cilantro
2/3 cup water
pepper
fresh herbs, to garnish

method

1 Cut the tops off the bell peppers and set aside. Discard the seeds from each pepper. Place the peppers in a large bowl and cover with boiling water. Let soak for 10 minutes then drain and set aside.

2 Heat a nonstick skillet and spray with the oil. Add the onion, garlic, ginger, and chiles and sauté for 3 minutes, stirring frequently. Sprinkle in the ground spices and continue to cook for an additional 2 minutes.

3 Remove the skillet from the heat and stir in the rice, carrot, zucchini, apricots, chopped cilantro, and pepper to taste. Stir well, then use to stuff the peppers.

4 Place the stuffed peppers in an ovenproof dish large enough to allow the peppers to stand upright. Put the reserved tops in position. Pour the water around their bases, cover loosely with the lid or foil, and cook in a preheated oven, 375°F/190°C, for 25–30 minutes, or until piping hot. Serve garnished with herbs.

stir-fried rice with green vegetables

ingredients

serves 4

8 oz/225 g/generous 1 cup
  jasmine rice
2 tbsp vegetable or peanut oil
1 tbsp green curry paste
6 scallions, sliced
2 garlic cloves, crushed
1 zucchini, cut into thin sticks
4 oz/115 g green beans
6 oz/175 g asparagus, trimmed
3–4 fresh Thai basil leaves

method

1 Cook the rice in lightly salted boiling water for 12–15 minutes, drain well, then cool thoroughly and chill overnight.

2 Heat the oil in a wok and stir-fry the curry paste for 1 minute. Add the scallions and garlic and stir-fry for 1 minute.

3 Add the zucchini, beans, and asparagus, and stir-fry for 3–4 minutes, until just tender. Break up the rice and add it to the wok. Cook, stirring constantly for 2–3 minutes, until the rice is hot. Stir in the basil leaves. Serve hot.

variation

Use red curry paste and red or orange vegetables such as red bell peppers and carrots to make a delicious variation to this recipe.

vegetable biryani

ingredients

serves 4

2 tbsp vegetable oil
3 whole cloves
3 cardamom pods, cracked
1 onion, chopped
4 oz/115 g carrots, chopped
2–3 garlic cloves, crushed
1–2 fresh red chiles, seeded
   and chopped
1-inch/2.5-cm piece fresh
   ginger, grated
4 oz/115 g cauliflower florets
6 oz/175 g broccoli florets
4 oz/115 g green beans, chopped
14 oz/400 g canned chopped
   tomatoes
5 fl oz/150 ml/²⁄₃ cup
   vegetable stock
salt and pepper
4 oz/115 g okra, sliced
1 tbsp chopped fresh cilantro,
   plus extra sprigs to garnish
4 oz/115 g/generous ½ cup brown
   basmati rice
few saffron threads (optional)
grated lime rind and cilantro sprigs,
   to garnish

method

1 Heat the oil in a large pan over low heat, add the spices, onion, carrots, garlic, chiles, and ginger and cook, stirring frequently, for 5 minutes.

2 Add the cauliflower, broccoli, and green beans and cook, stirring frequently, for 5 minutes. Stir in the tomatoes, stock, salt, and pepper and bring to a boil. Reduce the heat, cover, and let simmer for 10 minutes.

3 Add the okra and cook for an additional 8–10 minutes, or until the vegetables are tender. Stir in the cilantro. Strain off any excess liquid and keep warm.

4 Meanwhile, cook the rice with the saffron in a pan of lightly salted boiling water for 25 minutes, or until tender. Drain and keep warm.

5 Layer the vegetables and cooked rice in a deep dish or ovenproof bowl, packing the layers down firmly. Let stand for about 5 minutes, then invert on to a warmed serving dish and serve, garnished with grated lime rind and cilantro sprigs, with the reserved liquid.

vegetarian paella

ingredients

serves 4–6

½ tsp saffron threads
2 tbsp hot water
6 tbsp olive oil
1 Spanish onion, sliced
3 garlic cloves, minced
1 red bell pepper, seeded
   and sliced
1 orange bell pepper, seeded
   and sliced
1 large eggplant, cubed
7 oz/200 g/1 cup medium-grain
   paella rice
20 fl oz/625 ml/2½ cups
   vegetable stock
1 lb/450 g tomatoes, peeled
   and chopped
salt and pepper
4 oz/115 g mushrooms, sliced
4 oz/115 g green beans, halved
14 oz/400 g canned
   pinto beans

method

1 Put the saffron threads and water in a small bowl
   or cup and let infuse for a few minutes.

2 Meanwhile, heat the oil in a paella pan or wide, shallow
   skillet and cook the onion over medium heat, stirring,
   for 2–3 minutes, or until softened. Add the garlic, bell
   peppers, and eggplant and cook, stirring frequently,
   for 5 minutes.

3 Add the rice and cook, stirring constantly, for 1 minute,
   or until glossy and coated. Pour in the stock and add
   the tomatoes, saffron and its soaking water, salt, and
   pepper. Bring to a boil, then reduce the heat and
   let simmer, shaking the skillet frequently and stirring
   occasionally, for 15 minutes.

4 Stir in the mushrooms, green beans, and pinto beans
   with their can juices. Cook for an additional 10 minutes,
   then serve immediately.

artichoke paella

ingredients

serves 4–6

½ tsp saffron threads

2 tbsp hot water

3 tbsp olive oil

1 large onion, chopped

1 zucchini, coarsely chopped

2 garlic cloves, crushed

¼ tsp cayenne pepper

8 oz/225 g tomatoes, peeled
and cut into wedges

15 oz/425 g canned chickpeas,
drained

15 oz/425 g canned artichokes
hearts, drained and coarsely
sliced

12 oz/350 g/generous
1½ cups medium-grain
paella rice

42 fl oz/1.3 liters/5½ cups
simmering vegetable stock

5½ oz/150 g green beans,
blanched

salt and pepper

1 lemon, cut into wedges,
to serve

method

1 Put the saffron threads and water in a small bowl and let infuse for a few minutes.

2 Meanwhile, heat the oil in a paella pan and cook the onion and zucchini over medium heat, stirring, for 2–3 minutes, or until softened. Add the garlic, cayenne pepper, and saffron and its soaking liquid and cook, stirring constantly, for 1 minute. Add the tomato wedges, chickpeas, and artichokes and cook, stirring, for an additional 2 minutes.

3 Add the rice and cook, stirring constantly, for 1 minute, or until the rice is glossy and coated. Pour in most of the hot stock and bring to a boil, then let simmer, uncovered, for 10 minutes. Do not stir during cooking, but shake the pan once or twice. Add the green beans and season. Shake the pan and cook for 10–15 minutes, or until the rice grains are cooked. If the liquid is absorbed too quickly, pour in a little more hot stock, then shake the pan to spread the liquid through the paella.

4 When all the liquid has been absorbed and you detect a faint toasty aroma coming from the rice, remove from the heat immediately to prevent burning. Cover the pan with a clean dish towel or foil and let stand for 5 minutes. Serve direct from the pan with the lemon wedges to squeeze over the rice.

vegetables & salads

potato & cheese gratin

ingredients

serves 4–6

2 lb/900 g waxy potatoes, peeled
   and thinly sliced
1 large garlic clove, halved
butter, for greasing and dotting
   over the top
8 fl oz/225 ml/1 cup heavy cream
freshly grated nutmeg
salt and pepper
6 oz/175 g Gruyère cheese,
   finely grated

method

1 Put the potato slices in a bowl, cover with cold water and let stand for 5 minutes, then drain well.

2 Meanwhile, rub the bottom and sides of an oval gratin or ovenproof dish with the cut sides of the garlic halves, pressing down firmly to impart the flavor. Lightly grease the sides of the dish with butter.

3 Place the potatoes in a bowl with the cream and season with freshly grated nutmeg, salt, and pepper. Use your hands to mix everything together, then transfer the potatoes to the gratin dish and pour over any cream remaining in the bowl.

4 Sprinkle the cheese over the top and dot with butter. Place the gratin dish on a cookie sheet and bake in a preheated oven, 375°F/190°C, for 60–80 minutes, or until the potatoes are tender when pierced with a skewer and the top is golden and bubbling. Let stand for about 2 minutes, then serve straight from the gratin dish.

mushroom & cauliflower cheese crumble

ingredients

serves 4

1 medium cauliflower
55 g/2 oz/¼ cup butter
4 oz/115 g/1⅔ cups sliced white
    mushrooms
salt and pepper

for the topping

1⅔ cups dry breadcrumbs
2 tbsp grated Parmesan cheese
1 tsp dried oregano
1 tsp dried parsley
¼ cup butter

method

1 Bring a large pan of salted water to a boil. Break the cauliflower into small florets and cook in the boiling water for 3 minutes. Remove from the heat, drain well, and transfer to a large, shallow ovenproof dish.

2 Melt the butter in a small skillet over medium heat. Add the sliced mushrooms, stir to coat, and cook gently for 3 minutes. Remove from the heat and add to the cauliflower. Season with salt and pepper.

3 Combine the breadcrumbs, cheese, and herbs in a small mixing bowl, then sprinkle the crumbs over the vegetables.

4 Dice the butter for the topping and dot it over the crumbs. Place the dish in a preheated oven, 450°F/ 230°C, and bake for 15 minutes, or until the crumbs are golden brown and crisp. Serve from the dish.

leek & spinach pie

ingredients

serves 6–8

8 oz/225 g puff pastry
2 tbsp unsalted butter
2 leeks, sliced finely
8 oz/225 g spinach, chopped
2 eggs
10 fl oz/300 ml/1¼ cups
    heavy cream
pinch of dried thyme
salt and pepper

method

1 Roll the pastry into a rectangle about 10 x 12 inches/
25 x 30 cm. Let rest for 5 minutes, then press into a
8 x 10 inch/20 x 25 cm quiche pan. Do not trim the
overhang. Cover the pastry with aluminum foil and
chill in the refrigerator.

2 Melt the butter in a large skillet over medium heat.
Add the leeks, stir, and cook gently for 5 minutes, or
until soft. Add the spinach and cook for 3 minutes,
or until soft. Let cool.

3 Beat the eggs in a bowl. Stir in the cream and season
with thyme, salt, and pepper. Remove the pie shell
from the refrigerator and uncover. Spread the cooked
vegetables over the bottom. Pour in the egg mixture.

4 Place on a baking sheet and bake in a preheated oven,
350°F/180°C, for 30 minutes, or until set. Remove the
pie from the oven and let rest for 10 minutes before
removing from the baking sheet and serving.

potato, fontina & rosemary tart

ingredients

serves 4

10½ oz/300 g packet puff pastry
all-purpose flour, for dusting

filling

3–4 waxy potatoes
10½ oz/300 g Fontina cheese,
    cut into cubes
1 red onion, thinly sliced
3 large fresh rosemary sprigs
2 tbsp olive oil
salt and pepper
1 egg yolk

method

1 Roll out the dough on a lightly floured counter into a circle about 10 inches/25 cm in diameter and put on a cookie sheet.

2 Slice the potatoes as thinly as possible so that they are almost transparent—use a mandolin if you have one. Arrange the potato slices in a spiral, overlapping the slices to cover the pastry, leaving a ¾-inch/2-cm margin around the edge.

3 Arrange the cheese and onion over the potatoes, sprinkle with the rosemary, and drizzle over the oil. Season to taste with salt and pepper and brush the edges with the egg yolk to glaze.

4 Bake in a preheated oven, 375°F/190°C, for 25 minutes, or until the potatoes are tender and the pastry is brown and crisp. Serve hot.

caramelized onion tart

ingredients

serves 4–6

7 tbsp unsalted butter
1lb 5 oz/600 g onions, thinly sliced
2 eggs
3½ oz/100 g/scant ½ cup heavy
    cream
scant 1 cup grated Swiss cheese
8-inch/20-cm baked pie shell
3½ oz/100 g/generous 1 cup
    grated Parmesan cheese
salt and pepper

method

1 Melt the butter over medium heat in a heavy skillet. Stir in the onions and cook until they are well browned and caramelized. (This will take up to 30 minutes, depending on the width of the skillet.) Stir frequently to avoid burning. Remove the onions from the skillet and set aside.

2 Beat the eggs in a large mixing bowl, stir in the cream, and season with salt and pepper. Add the Swiss cheese and mix well. Mix in the cooked onions.

3 Pour the egg and onion mixture into the baked pie shell, sprinkle with Parmesan, and place on a baking sheet. Bake in a preheated oven, 375°F/190°C, for 15–20 minutes, or until the filling has set and begun to brown.

4 Remove from the oven and let rest for at least 10 minutes. The tart can be served hot or let cool to room temperature.

stuffed baked potatoes

ingredients

serves 4

2 lb/900 g baking potatoes,
    scrubbed
2 tbsp vegetable oil
1 tsp coarse sea salt
4 oz/115 g/½ cup butter
1 small onion, chopped
salt and pepper
4 oz/115 g/1 cup grated
    Cheddar cheese or
    crumbled blue cheese
snipped fresh chives,
    to garnish

optional

4 tbsp canned, drained
    corn kernels
4 tbsp cooked mushrooms,
    zucchini, or bell peppers

method

1 Prick the potatoes in several places with a fork and put on a cookie sheet. Brush with the oil and sprinkle with the salt. Bake in a preheated oven, 375°F/190°C, for 1 hour, or until the skins are crispy and the insides are soft when pierced with a fork.

2 Meanwhile, melt 1 tablespoon of the butter in a small skillet over medium-low heat. Add the onion and cook, stirring occasionally, for 8–10 minutes until soft and golden. Set aside.

3 Cut the potatoes in half lengthwise. Scoop the flesh into a large bowl, leaving the skins intact. Set aside the skins. Increase the oven temperature to 400°F/200°C.

4 Coarsely mash the potato flesh and mix in the onion and remaining butter. Add salt and pepper to taste and stir in any of the optional ingredients. Spoon the mixture back into the reserved potato skins. Top the potatoes with the cheese.

5 Cook the filled potato skins in the oven for 10 minutes, or until the cheese has melted and is beginning to brown. Garnish with chives and serve immediately.

roasted ratatouille & potato wedges

ingredients

serves 4

10¹/₂ oz/300 g potatoes in their
    skins, scrubbed
7 oz/200 g eggplant, cut into
    ¹/₂-inch/1-cm wedges
4¹/₂ oz/125 g red onion, cut into
    ¹/₄-inch/5-mm slices
7 oz/200 g seeded bell peppers,
    sliced into ¹/₂-inch/1-cm strips
6 oz/175 g zucchini, cut into
    ¹/₂-inch/1-cm slices
4¹/₂ oz/125 g cherry tomatoes
3¹/₄ oz/90 g lowfat cream cheese
1 tsp runny honey
pinch of smoked paprika
1 tsp chopped fresh parsley

marinade

1 tsp fresh rosemary
1 tbsp fresh lemon thyme
1 tsp vegetable oil
1 tbsp lemon juice
4 tbsp white wine
1 tsp sugar
2 tbsp chopped fresh basil
¹/₄ tsp smoked paprika

method

1 Bake the potatoes in a preheated oven, 400°F/200°C, for 30 minutes, then remove and cut into wedges—the flesh should not be completely cooked.

2 To make the marinade, finely chop the rosemary and lemon thyme, then place all the ingredients in a bowl and blend with a hand-held electric blender until smooth, or use a food processor.

3 Put the potato wedges into a large bowl with the eggplant, onion, bell peppers, and zucchini, then pour over the marinade and mix thoroughly.

4 Arrange the vegetables on a nonstick baking tray and roast in the oven, turning occasionally, for 25–30 minutes, or until golden brown and tender. Add the tomatoes for the last 5 minutes of the cooking time, just to split the skins and warm slightly.

5 Mix the cream cheese, honey, and paprika together in a bowl.

6 Serve the vegetables with the cream cheese mixture, and sprinkled with chopped parsley.

vegetable chili

ingredients

serves 4

1 eggplant, cut into
   1-inch/2.5-cm slices
1 tbsp olive oil, plus extra for
   brushing
1 large red onion, finely chopped
2 red or yellow bell peppers,
   seeded and finely chopped
3–4 garlic cloves, finely chopped
   or crushed
1 lb 12 oz/800 g canned chopped
   tomatoes
1 tbsp mild chili powder
½ tsp ground cumin
½ tsp dried oregano
2 small zucchini, cut into quarters,
   lengthwise, and sliced
14 oz/400 g canned kidney beans,
   drained and rinsed
16 fl oz/450 ml/2 cups water
1 tbsp tomato paste
6 scallions, finely chopped
generous 1 cup grated
   Cheddar cheese
salt and pepper

method

1 Brush the eggplant slices on one side with olive oil. Heat half the oil in a large, heavy-bottomed skillet over medium–high heat. Add the eggplant slices, oiled-side up, and cook for 5–6 minutes, or until browned on one side. Turn the slices over, cook on the other side until browned, and transfer to a plate. Cut into bite-size pieces.

2 Heat the remaining oil in a large pan over medium heat. Add the onion and bell peppers and cook, stirring occasionally, for 3–4 minutes, or until the onion is softened, but not browned.

3 Add the garlic and cook for an additional 2–3 minutes, or until the onion is beginning to color.

4 Add the tomatoes, chili powder, cumin, and oregano. Season to taste with salt and pepper. Bring just to a boil, reduce the heat, cover, and simmer gently for 15 minutes.

5 Add the zucchini, eggplant pieces, and kidney beans. Stir in the water and the tomato paste. Return to a boil, then cover and continue simmering for 45 minutes, or until the vegetables are tender. Taste and adjust the seasoning if necessary. Ladle into warmed serving bowls and top with scallions and cheese.

cherry tomato clafoutis

ingredients

serves 4–6

14 oz/400 g cherry tomatoes
3 tbsp chopped fresh flat-leaf
    parsley, snipped fresh chives,
    or finely shredded fresh basil
3½ oz/100 g/1 cup grated
    Gruyère cheese
2 oz/55 g/generous ⅓ cup
    all-purpose flour
4 large eggs, lightly beaten
3 tbsp sour cream
8 fl oz/225 ml/1 cup milk
salt and pepper

method

1 Lightly grease an oval ovenproof dish. Arrange the cherry tomatoes in the dish and sprinkle with the herbs and half the cheese.

2 Put the flour in a mixing bowl, then slowly add the eggs, whisking until smooth. Whisk in the sour cream, then slowly whisk in the milk to make a thin, smooth batter. Season with salt and pepper.

3 Gently pour the batter over the tomatoes, then sprinkle the top with the remaining cheese. Bake in a preheated oven, 375°F/190°C, for 40–45 minutes, or until set and puffy, covering the top with foil if it browns too much before the batter sets. If serving hot, let the clafoutis cool for a few minutes before cutting, or let cool to room temperature.

cheese baked zucchini

ingredients

serves 4

4 medium zucchini

2 tbsp extra virgin olive oil

4 oz/115 g mozzarella cheese, sliced thinly

2 large tomatoes, seeded and diced

2 tsp chopped fresh basil or oregano

method

1 Slice the zucchini lengthwise into 4 strips each. Brush with oil and place on a baking sheet.

2 Bake the zucchini in a preheated oven, 400°F/200°C, for 10 minutes without letting them get too floppy.

3 Remove the zucchini from the oven. Arrange the slices of cheese on top and sprinkle with diced tomato and basil or oregano. Return to the oven for 5 minutes, or until the cheese melts.

4 Remove the zucchini from the oven and transfer carefully to serving plates.

tomato pizza

ingredients

serves 4–6

9-inch/23-cm ready-made
   pizza base
fresh basil leaves, torn

tomato topping

²/₃ cup crushed tomatoes
3 tbsp tomato paste
2 garlic cloves, crushed
pinch each of sugar, salt,
   and pepper
handful of cherry tomatoes

cheese topping (optional)

²/₃ cup crushed tomatoes
3 tbsp tomato paste
4 oz/115 g jar roasted bell peppers,
   drained and thickly sliced
a few black olives
salt and pepper
4 oz/115 g firm mozzarella
   cheese, grated
2 oz/55 g Parmesan cheese, grated

method

1 To make the tomato topping, mix the crushed tomatoes, tomato paste, garlic, sugar, and salt and pepper together in a bowl. Spread over the ready-made pizza base and scatter with the cherry tomatoes.

2 To make the cheese topping, if wished, mix the crushed tomatoes and tomato paste together in a bowl and spread over the pizza base. Top with the peppers and the olives. Season with salt and pepper and scatter the mozzarella and Parmesan cheeses over the top.

3 Bake in a preheated oven, 400°F/200°C, for 8–10 minutes until hot and bubbling. Scatter with basil leaves and serve immediately.

variation

You can add different toppings to this basic pizza to create many variations, for example mushrooms and pineapple for a tropical pizza, or spicy chiles for a hot pizza—the combinations are endless!

broccoli & sesame frittata

ingredients

serves 2

6 oz/175 g broccoli, broken
    into small florets
3 oz/85 g asparagus spears,
    sliced diagonally
1 tbsp virgin olive oil
1 onion, cut into small wedges
2–4 garlic cloves, finely chopped
1 large orange bell pepper, seeded
    and chopped
4 eggs
3 tbsp cold water
salt and pepper
1 oz/25 g/⅛ cup sesame seeds
½ oz/15 g/⅛ cup freshly grated
    Parmesan cheese
3 scallions, finely sliced

method

1 Cook the broccoli in a pan of lightly salted boiling water
for 4 minutes. Add the asparagus after 2 minutes. Drain,
then plunge into cold water. Drain again and set aside.

2 Heat the oil in a large skillet over low heat, add the
onion, garlic, and orange bell pepper and cook,
stirring frequently, for 8 minutes, or until the
vegetables have softened.

3 Beat the eggs with the water, salt, and pepper in a
medium-size bowl. Pour into the skillet, add the
broccoli and asparagus, and stir gently. Cook over
medium heat for 3–4 minutes, drawing the mixture
from the edges of the skillet into the center, allowing
the uncooked egg to flow to the edges of the skillet.
Preheat the broiler.

4 Sprinkle the top of the frittata with the sesame seeds
and cheese and cook under the preheated broiler for
3–5 minutes, or until golden and set. Sprinkle with
the scallions, cut into wedges, and serve. Serve warm
or cold.

zucchini, carrot & tomato frittata

ingredients

serves 4

2 sprays olive oil
1 onion, cut into small wedges
1–2 garlic cloves, crushed
2 eggs
2 egg whites
1 zucchini, about 3 oz/85 g,
    trimmed and grated
2 carrots, about 4 oz/115 g,
    peeled and grated
2 tomatoes, chopped
pepper
1 tbsp shredded fresh basil,
    for sprinkling

method

1 Heat the oil in a large nonstick skillet, add the onion and garlic, and sauté for 5 minutes, stirring frequently. Beat the eggs and egg whites together in a bowl then pour into the skillet. Using a spatula or fork, pull the egg mixture from the sides of the skillet into the center, allowing the uncooked egg to take its place.

2 Once the base has set lightly, add the grated zucchini and carrots with the tomatoes. Add pepper to taste and continue to cook over low heat until the eggs are set to personal preference.

3 Sprinkle with the shredded basil, cut the frittata into quarters and serve.

mushroom stroganoff

ingredients

serves 4

1 lb 4 oz/550 g mixed fresh
    mushrooms, such as cremini,
    chanterelles, porcini, and oyster
1 red onion, diced
2 garlic cloves, crushed
15 fl oz/425ml/scant 2 cups
    vegetable stock
1 tbsp tomato paste
2 tbsp lemon juice
scant tbsp cornstarch
2 tbsp cold water
4oz/115g/½ cup lowfat
    plain yogurt
3 tbsp chopped fresh parsley
pepper
boiled brown or white rice and
    crisp green salad, to serve

method

1 Put the mushrooms, onion, garlic, stock, tomato paste, and lemon juice into a pan and bring to a boil. Reduce the heat, cover, and let simmer for 15 minutes, or until the onion is tender.

2 Blend the cornstarch with the water in a small bowl and stir into the mushroom mixture. Return to a boil, stirring constantly, and cook until the sauce thickens. Reduce the heat and let simmer for an additional 2 minutes, stirring occasionally.

3 Just before serving, remove the pan from the heat, and stir in the yogurt, making sure that the stroganoff is not boiling or it may separate and curdle. Stir in 2 tablespoons of the parsley and season with pepper. Transfer the stroganoff to a warmed serving dish, sprinkle over the remaining parsley, and serve at once with boiled brown or white rice and a crisp green salad.

thai yellow vegetable curry with brown basmati rice

ingredients

serves 4

1¾oz/50 g bell pepper, seeded
1¾oz/50 g celery
1¾oz/50 g baby corn
3 oz/85 g leek
3½oz/100 g sweet potato
3½oz/100 g bok choy
1¾oz/50 g zucchini
1¾oz/50 g snow peas
10 fl oz/300 ml/1¼ cups
   pineapple juice
7 fl oz/200 ml/scant 1 cup water
3 tbsp lime juice
2 tbsp cornstarch
4 tbsp lowfat plain yogurt
4 tbsp chopped fresh cilantro
5½oz/150 g cooked brown
   basmati rice

spice mix

1 tsp finely chopped garlic
¼tsp ground turmeric
1 tsp ground coriander
1 tsp finely chopped lemongrass
3 kaffir lime leaves
1 tsp finely chopped green chile

method

1 To make the spice mix, pound all the spices to a fine paste using a mortar and pestle.

2 To prepare the vegetables, cut the bell pepper into ½-inch/1-cm squares, cut the celery, baby corn, and leek into ¼-inch/5-mm lengths, and cut the sweet potato into ½-inch/1-cm cubes. Shred the bok choy. Cut the zucchini into ¼-inch/5-mm cubes and slice the snow peas into thin strips.

3 Put the bell pepper, celery, baby corn, leek, sweet potato, pineapple juice, water, and the spice mix into a large pan with a lid and bring to a boil. Reduce the heat and skim the scum from the surface with a metal spoon. Cover and let simmer for 15 minutes.

4 Add the bok choy, zucchini, and snow peas and cook for 2 minutes. Add the lime juice, then gradually add the cornstarch blended with a little cold water. Cook the curry, stirring constantly, until thickened to the required consistency.

5 Remove the curry from the heat and let cool for 2–3 minutes. Stir in the yogurt. (Do not boil once the yogurt has been added or the curry will separate.) Stir in the fresh cilantro and serve the curry with the rice.

roasted garlic mashed potatoes

ingredients

serves 4

2 whole garlic bulbs
1 tbsp olive oil
2 lb/900 g mealy potatoes, peeled
4 fl oz/125 ml/½ cup milk
2 oz/55 g butter
salt and pepper

method

1 Separate the garlic cloves, place on a large piece of foil, and drizzle with the oil. Wrap the garlic in the foil and roast in a preheated oven, 350°F/180°C, for about 1 hour, or until very tender. Let cool slightly.

2 Meanwhile, cut the potatoes into chunks, then cook in a pan of lightly salted boiling water for 15 minutes, or until tender.

3 Squeeze the cooled garlic cloves out of their skins and push through a strainer into a pan. Add the milk and butter and season with salt and pepper. Heat gently until the butter has melted.

4 Drain the cooked potatoes, then mash in the pan until smooth. Pour in the garlic mixture and heat gently, stirring, until the ingredients are combined. Serve hot.

roasted squash wedges

ingredients

serves 4

7 oz/200 g acorn squash
or other type of squash, peeled,
seeded, and cut into 4 wedges
1 tsp vegetable oil
3½ oz/100 g onion, finely chopped
1 tsp minced garlic
2½ oz/70 g three-grain risotto mix
(baldo rice, spelt, and pearl
barley—this is available
ready-mixed)
10 fl oz/300 ml/1¼ cups
vegetable stock
8 oz/225 g asparagus tips
2 tbsp finely chopped fresh
marjoram, plus extra
to garnish
3 tbsp lowfat cream cheese
2 tbsp finely chopped
fresh parsley
pepper

method

1 Spread out the squash wedges on a nonstick cookie sheet and roast in a preheated oven, 400°F/200°C, for 20 minutes, or until the wedges are tender and golden brown.

2 Meanwhile, heat the oil in a medium pan over high heat, add the onion and garlic, and cook, stirring, until softened but not colored. Add the risotto mix and stir in half the stock. Let simmer, stirring occasionally, until the stock has reduced in the pan. Pour in the remaining stock and continue to cook, stirring occasionally, until the grains are tender.

3 Cut 6 oz/175g of the asparagus into 4-inch/10-cm lengths and blanch in a pan of boiling water for 2 minutes. Drain and keep warm. Cut the remaining asparagus into ¼-inch/5-mm slices and add to the risotto for the last 3 minutes of the cooking time.

4 Remove the risotto from the heat and stir in the marjoram, cream cheese, and parsley. Season with pepper. Do not reboil.

5 To serve, lay the squash wedges on warmed serving plates, then spoon over the risotto and top with the asparagus. Garnish with marjoram.

colcannon

ingredients

serves 4

8 oz/225 g green cabbage,
    shredded
5 tbsp milk
8 oz/225 g/1½ cups diced
    mealy potatoes
1 large leek, chopped
pinch of grated nutmeg
1 tbsp butter, melted
salt and pepper

method

1 Cook the shredded cabbage in a pan of boiling salted water for 7–10 minutes. Drain thoroughly and set aside.

2 Meanwhile, in a separate pan, bring the milk to a boil and add the potatoes and leek. Reduce the heat and simmer for 15–20 minutes, or until they are cooked through.

3 Stir in the grated nutmeg and thoroughly mash the potatoes and leek together.

4 Add the drained cabbage to the mashed potato and leek mixture and mix well.

5 Spoon the mixture into a warmed serving dish, making a hollow in the center with the back of a spoon.

6 Pour the melted butter into the hollow and serve the colcannon immediately.

stir-fried broccoli

ingredients

serves 4

2 tbsp vegetable oil
2 broccoli heads, cut into florets
2 tbsp soy sauce
1 tsp cornstarch
1 tbsp superfine sugar
1 tsp grated fresh ginger
1 garlic clove, crushed
pinch of dried red chile flakes
1 tsp toasted sesame seeds,
    to garnish

method

1 Heat the oil in a large preheated wok or skillet over high heat until almost smoking. Add the broccoli and stir-fry for 4–5 minutes. Reduce the heat to medium.

2 Combine the soy sauce, cornstarch, sugar, ginger, garlic, and red chile flakes in a small bowl. Add the mixture to the broccoli and cook, stirring constantly, for 2–3 minutes until the sauce thickens slightly.

3 Transfer to a warmed serving dish, garnish with the sesame seeds, and serve immediately.

roasted onions

ingredients

serves 4

8 large onions, peeled
3 tbsp olive oil
2 oz/55 g butter
2 tsp chopped fresh thyme
salt and pepper
7 oz/200 g/1 cup Cheddar
   cheese, grated

method

1 Cut a cross down through the top of the onions towards the root, without cutting all the way through. Place the onions in a roasting pan and drizzle over the olive oil.

2 Press a little of the butter into the open crosses, sprinkle with the thyme, and season with salt and pepper. Cover with foil and roast in a preheated oven, 350°F/180°C, for 40–45 minutes.

3 Remove from the oven, take off the foil and baste the onions with the pan juices. Return to the oven and cook for a further 15 minutes, uncovered, to allow the onions to brown.

4 Take the onions out of the oven and scatter the grated cheese over them. Return them to the oven for a few minutes so that the cheese starts to melt over the top. Serve immediately.

brussels sprouts with chestnuts

ingredients

serves 4

1 lb/450 g Brussels sprouts
4 oz/115 g/½ cup unsalted butter
2 oz/55 g/generous ¼ cup
　　brown sugar
4 oz/115 g cooked and peeled
　　chestnuts

method

1 Trim the Brussels sprouts and remove and discard any loose outer leaves. Add to a large pan of boiling salted water and boil for 5–10 minutes until just tender, but not too soft. Drain well, refresh under cold water, and drain again. Set aside.

2 Melt the butter in a heavy-bottom skillet over medium heat. Add the sugar and stir until dissolved. Add the chestnuts and cook, stirring occasionally, until well coated and beginning to brown.

3 Add the sprouts to the chestnuts and mix well. Reduce the heat and cook gently, stirring occasionally, for 3–4 minutes to heat through.

4 Remove from the heat, transfer to a warmed serving dish, and serve immediately.

tabbouleh

ingredients

serves 4

6 oz/175 g/scant 1 cup
    bulgur wheat
3 tbsp extra-virgin olive oil
4 tbsp lemon juice
salt and pepper
4 scallions
1 green bell pepper,
    seeded and sliced
4 tomatoes, chopped
2 tbsp chopped fresh parsley
2 tbsp chopped fresh mint
8 black olives, pitted

method

1 Place the bulgur wheat in a large bowl and add enough cold water to cover. Let stand for 30 minutes, or until the wheat has doubled in size. Drain well and press out as much liquid as possible. Spread out the wheat on paper towels to dry.

2 Place the wheat in a serving bowl. Mix the olive oil and lemon juice together in a pitcher and season with salt and pepper. Pour the lemon mixture over the wheat and let marinate for 1 hour.

3 Using a sharp knife, finely chop the scallions, then add to the salad with the green bell pepper, tomatoes, parsley, and mint and toss lightly to mix. Top the salad with the olives and serve immediately.

greek salad

ingredients

serves 4

4 tomatoes, cut into wedges
1 onion, sliced
½ cucumber, sliced
8 oz/225 g/1½ cups kalamata
    olives, stoned
8 oz/225 g Feta cheese, cubed
2 tbsp fresh cilantro leaves
fresh flat-leaf parsley sprigs,
    to garnish
pita bread, to serve

dressing

5 tbsp extra-virgin olive oil
2 tbsp white wine vinegar
1 tbsp lemon juice
½ tsp sugar
1 tbsp chopped fresh cilantro
salt and pepper

method

1 To make the dressing, put all the ingredients for the dressing into a large bowl and mix well together.

2 Add the tomatoes, onion, cucumber, olives, cheese, and cilantro. Toss all the ingredients together, then divide between individual serving bowls. Garnish with parsley sprigs and serve with pita bread.

roasted bell pepper salad

ingredients

serves 8

3 red bell peppers
3 yellow bell peppers
5 tbsp Spanish extra-virgin olive oil
2 tbsp dry sherry vinegar or
    lemon juice
2 garlic cloves, crushed
pinch of sugar
salt and pepper
1 tbsp capers
8 small black Spanish olives
2 tbsp chopped fresh marjoram,
    plus extra sprigs to garnish

method

1 Preheat the broiler to high. Place the bell peppers on a wire rack or broiler pan and cook under the broiler for 10 minutes, until their skins have blackened and blistered, turning them frequently.

2 Remove the roasted bell peppers from the heat, and either put them in a bowl and cover tightly with a clean, damp dish towel, or put them in a plastic bag. The steam helps to soften the skins and makes it easier to remove them. Let stand for about 15 minutes, until cool enough to handle.

3 Holding one bell pepper at a time over a clean bowl, make a small hole in the base and gently squeeze out the juices and reserve them. Still holding the bell pepper over the bowl, carefully peel off the blackened skin with your fingers, or a knife, and discard it. Cut the bell peppers in half and remove the stem, core, and seeds, then cut each bell pepper into neat thin strips. Arrange the bell pepper strips on a serving dish.

4 To the reserved pepper juices add the olive oil, sherry vinegar, garlic, sugar, salt, and pepper. Whisk together until combined. Drizzle the dressing over the salad.

5 Sprinkle the capers, olives, and chopped marjoram over the salad, garnish with marjoram sprigs, and serve at room temperature.

moroccan tomato
& red bell pepper salad

ingredients

serves 4

3 red bell peppers
4 ripe tomatoes
½ bunch of fresh cilantro, chopped
2 garlic cloves, finely chopped
salt and pepper

method

1 Preheat the broiler. Place the bell peppers on a baking sheet and cook under the broiler, turning occasionally, for 15 minutes. Add the tomatoes and broil, turning occasionally, for an additional 5–10 minutes, or until all the skins are charred and blistered. Remove from the heat and let cool.

2 Peel and seed the bell peppers and tomatoes and slice the flesh thinly. Place in a bowl, mix well, and season with salt and pepper. Sprinkle with the cilantro and garlic, cover with plastic wrap, and chill in the refrigerator for at least 1 hour. Just before serving, drain off any excess liquid.

green bean salad with feta cheese

ingredients

serves 4

12 oz/350 g green beans
1 red onion, chopped
3–4 tbsp chopped fresh cilantro
2 radishes, thinly sliced
2¾ oz/75 g Feta cheese drained
    weight, crumbled
1 tsp chopped fresh oregano,
    plus extra leaves to garnish
    (optional), or ½ tsp dried
    oregano
pepper
2 tbsp red wine or fruit vinegar
3 fl oz/80 ml/⅓ cup extra virgin
    olive oil
3 ripe tomatoes, cut into wedges
slices of crusty bread, to serve

method

1 Bring about 2 inches/5 cm of water to a boil in the bottom of a steamer. Add the beans to the top part of the steamer, cover, and steam for 5 minutes, or until just tender.

2 Place the beans in a large bowl and add the onion, cilantro, radishes, and Feta cheese.

3 Sprinkle the oregano over the salad, then season with pepper. Mix the vinegar and oil together in a small bowl and pour over the salad. Toss gently to mix well.

4 Transfer to a serving platter, surround with the tomato wedges, and serve at once with slices of crusty bread, or cover and chill until ready to serve.

nutty beet salad

ingredients

serves 4

3 tbsp red wine vinegar
    or fruit vinegar
3 cooked beets, grated
2 sharp eating apples
2 tbsp lemon juice
4 large handfuls mixed salad
    greens, to serve
4 tbsp pecans, to garnish

for the dressing

2 fl oz/50 ml/¼ cup plain yogurt
2 fl oz/50 ml/¼ cup mayonnaise
1 garlic clove, chopped
1 tbsp chopped fresh dill
salt and pepper

method

1 Sprinkle vinegar over the beets, cover with plastic wrap, and chill for at least 4 hours.

2 Core and slice the apples, place the slices in a dish, and sprinkle with the lemon juice.

3 Combine the dressing ingredients in a small bowl. Remove the beets from the refrigerator and dress. Add the apples to the beets and mix gently to coat with the salad dressing.

4 To serve, arrange a handful of salad greens on each plate and top with a large spoonful of the apple and beet mixture.

5 Toast the pecans in a heavy, dry skillet over medium heat for 2 minutes, or until they begin to brown. Sprinkle them over the beets and apple to garnish.

warm goat cheese mixed leaf salad

ingredients

serves 4

1 small Iceberg lettuce, torn
    into pieces
handful of arugula leaves
few radicchio leaves, torn
6 slices French bread
4 oz/115 g goat cheese, sliced

for the dressing
4 tbsp extra virgin olive oil
1 tbsp white wine vinegar
salt and pepper

method

1 Preheat the broiler. Divide all the leaves among 4 individual salad bowls.

2 Toast one side of the bread under the broiler until golden. Place a slice of cheese on top of each untoasted side and toast the bread until the cheese is just melting.

3 Put all the dressing ingredients into a bowl and beat together until combined. Pour over the leaves, tossing to coat.

4 Cut each slice of bread in half and place 3 halves on top of each salad. Toss very gently to combine and serve warm.

red onion, tomato & herb salad

ingredients

serves 4

2 lb/900 g tomatoes, sliced thinly
1 tbsp sugar (optional)
1 red onion, sliced thinly
large handful coarsely chopped
    fresh herbs
salt and pepper

for the dressing

2–4 tbsp vegetable oil
2 tbsp red wine vinegar
    or fruit vinegar

method

1 Arrange the tomato slices in a shallow bowl. Sprinkle with sugar (if using), salt, and pepper.

2 Separate the onion slices into rings and sprinkle them over the tomatoes. Sprinkle the herbs over the top. Any fresh herbs that are in season can be used—for example, tarragon, sorrel, cilantro, or basil.

3 Place the dressing ingredients in a jar with a screw-top lid. Shake well. Pour the dressing over the salad and mix gently.

4 Cover with plastic wrap and chill for 20 minutes. Remove the salad from the refrigerator 5 minutes before serving, unwrap the dish, and stir gently before setting out on the table.

desserts

rich vanilla ice cream

ingredients

serves 4–6

10 fl oz/300 ml/1¼ cups light
　cream and 10 fl oz/300 ml/
　1¼ cups heavy cream or
　20 fl oz/625 ml/2½ cups
　heavy whipping cream
1 vanilla bean
4 large egg yolks
3½ oz/100 g/generous ½ cup
　superfine sugar

method

1 Pour the light and heavy cream or heavy whipping cream into a large heavy-bottom pan. Split open the vanilla bean and scrape out the seeds into the cream, then add the whole vanilla bean too. Bring almost to a boil, then remove from the heat and let infuse for 30 minutes.

2 Put the egg yolks and sugar in a large bowl and whisk together until pale and the mixture leaves a trail when the whisk is lifted. Remove the vanilla bean from the cream, then slowly add the cream to the egg mixture, stirring all the time with a wooden spoon. Strain the mixture into the rinsed-out pan or a double boiler and cook over low heat for 10–15 minutes, stirring all the time, until the mixture thickens enough to coat the back of the spoon. Do not let the mixture boil or it will curdle.

3 Remove the custard from the heat and let cool for at least 1 hour, stirring from time to time to prevent a skin forming.

4 Churn the custard in an ice-cream maker following the manufacturer's instructions. Serve immediately if wished, or transfer to a freezerproof container, cover with a lid, and store in the freezer.

lemon yogurt ice cream

ingredients

serves 4–6

2–3 lemons
20 fl oz/625 ml/scant 2½ cups
    strained plain yogurt
5 fl oz/150 ml/²⁄₃ cup
    heavy cream
3½ oz/100 g/½ cup superfine sugar
finely pared orange zest,
    to garnish

method

1 Squeeze the juice from the lemons—you need
6 tablespoons in total. Put the juice into a bowl, add
the yogurt, cream, and sugar, and mix well together.

2 If using an ice-cream machine, churn the mixture in
the machine following the manufacturer's instructions.
Alternatively, freeze the mixture in a freezerproof
container, uncovered, for 1–2 hours, or until it starts
to set around the edges.

3 Turn the mixture into a bowl and stir with a fork or beat
in a food processor until smooth. Return to the freezer
and freeze for an additional 2–3 hours, or until firm or
required. Cover the container with a lid for storing.
Serve with finely pared orange zest.

raspberry ripple ice cream

ingredients

serves 6

3 oz/85 g/³/₈ cup fresh or frozen
raspberries, thawed if frozen,
plus extra to serve

2 tbsp water

2 eggs

½ oz/20 g/1 tbsp superfine sugar

10 fl oz/300 ml/1¼ cups
milk, warmed

1 tsp vanilla extract

10 fl oz/300 ml/1¼ cups heavy
cream

method

1 Turn the freezer to rapid. Put the raspberries into a pan
with the water and bring to a boil, then reduce the heat
and let simmer gently for 5 minutes. Remove from the
heat and let cool for 30 minutes. Transfer to a food
processor or blender and process to a purée, then rub
through a nylon strainer to remove the pips. Set aside.

2 Beat the eggs in a bowl. Stir the sugar into the
warmed milk, then slowly pour onto the eggs, beating
constantly. Strain into a clean pan and cook over low
heat, stirring constantly, for 8–10 minutes, or until
the custard thickens and coats the back of a wooden
spoon. Add the vanilla extract, remove from the heat,
and let cool.

3 Half-whip the cream in a large bowl, then slowly stir in
the cooled custard. Pour into a freezerproof container
and freeze for 1½ hours, or until starting to set around
the outside. Remove from the freezer and stir the
mixture, breaking up any ice crystals.

4 Return the mixture to the freezer and freeze for an
additional hour, then remove from the freezer again
and gently stir in the raspberry purée to give a rippled
effect. Return to the freezer for an hour or until frozen.
Serve in scoops with extra fresh raspberries.

icy fruit blizzard

ingredients

serves 4

1 pineapple, peeled, cored, and cut into chunks

1 large piece seeded watermelon, peeled and cut into small pieces

8 oz/225 g/1½ cups strawberries or other berries, hulled and left whole or sliced

1 mango, peach, or nectarine, peeled and sliced

1 banana, peeled and sliced

orange juice

superfine sugar, to taste

method

1 Cover 2 nonstick cookie sheets or ordinary cookie sheets with a sheet of plastic wrap. Arrange the fruits on top and open freeze for at least 2 hours, or until firm and icy.

2 Place one type of fruit in a food processor and process until it is all broken up into small pieces.

3 Add a little orange juice and sugar to taste, and continue to process until it forms a granular mixture. Repeat with the remaining fruits. Arrange in chilled bowls and serve immediately.

blueberry frozen yogurt

ingredients

serves 4

6 oz/175g/¾ cup fresh blueberries
finely grated rind and juice of
    1 orange
3 tbsp maple syrup
1 lb 2 oz/500 g plain lowfat yogurt

method

1 Put the blueberries, orange rind and juice into a food processor or blender and process to a purée. Strain through a nylon strainer into a bowl or pitcher.

2 Stir the maple syrup and yogurt together in a large mixing bowl, then fold in the fruit purée.

3 Churn the mixture in an ice-cream machine, following the manufacturer's instructions, then freeze for 5–6 hours. If you don't have an ice-cream machine, transfer the mixture to a freezerproof container, and freeze for 2 hours.

4 Remove from the freezer, turn out into a bowl, and beat until smooth. Return to the freezer and freeze until firm.

apricot & passion fruit sorbet

ingredients

serves 6

sorbet

3½oz/100 g no-soak dried apricots
9 fl oz/250 ml/generous
   1 cup water
2 tbsp freshly squeezed
   lemon juice
2 tbsp freshly squeezed
   orange juice
7 tbsp passion fruit pulp, strained
   to remove the seeds

sesame snaps

1 tbsp sesame seeds
1 tbsp liquid glucose
3 tbsp superfine sugar
2 tbsp all-purpose flour

method

1 To make the sorbet, put the apricots in a pan with the water and bring to a boil. Reduce the heat and let simmer for 10–15 minutes, or until soft. Remove from the heat. Purée the apricots in a food processor with the water, then blend in the lemon juice, orange juice, and 3 tbsp of the passion fruit pulp.

2 Add 2 tbsp of the passion fruit pulp, mix well, then transfer to a large, freezerproof container and freeze for 20 minutes. Beat the sorbet to break down the ice crystals, then return to the freezer. Freeze for 2 hours, or until fully frozen, beating every 20 minutes to give a smooth texture to the finished sorbet.

3 To make the sesame snaps, toss the sesame seeds in a small pan over high heat until golden brown. Remove from the heat, add the glucose, sugar, and flour and mix with a metal spoon to form a sticky paste. Remove from the pan and let cool slightly. Roll the paste into a sausage shape and cut into 16 pieces. With wet hands, roll each piece into a small ball, then lightly press out on to a sheet of silicone.

4 Bake in a preheated oven, 350°F/180°C, for 6 minutes until golden brown. Transfer to a wire rack and let cool. Serve the sorbet with the remaining passion fruit pulp spooned over and the sesame snaps to accompany.

spanish caramel custard

ingredients

serves 6

18 fl oz/500 ml/scant
2½ cups whole milk
½ orange with 2 long, thin pieces
of zest pared off and reserved
1 vanilla bean, split, or
½ tsp vanilla extract
6 oz/175 g/scant 1 cup
superfine sugar
butter, for greasing the dish
3 large eggs, plus 2 large egg yolks

method

1 Pour the milk into a pan with the orange zest and vanilla bean or extract. Bring to a boil, then remove from the heat and stir in 3 oz/85g/½ cup of the sugar; set aside for at least 30 minutes to infuse.

2 Meanwhile, put the remaining sugar and 4 tablespoons of water in another pan over medium-high heat. Stir until the sugar dissolves, then boil without stirring until the caramel turns deep golden brown. Immediately remove the pan from the heat and squeeze in a few drops of orange juice to stop the cooking. Pour into a lightly buttered 32-fl oz/1-liter/5-cup soufflé dish and swirl to cover the base; set aside.

3 Return the pan of infused milk to the heat, and bring to a simmer. Beat the whole eggs and egg yolks together in a heatproof bowl. Pour the warm milk into the eggs, whisking constantly. Strain into the soufflé dish.

4 Place the soufflé dish in a roasting pan and pour in enough boiling water to come halfway up the sides of the dish. Bake in a preheated oven, 325°F/160°C, for up to 90 minutes until set. Remove the soufflé dish from the roasting pan and set aside to cool. Cover and let chill overnight. To serve, run a metal spatula round the set custard, then invert onto a serving plate, shaking firmly to release.

creamy mango brûlée

ingredients

serves 4

2 mangoes
9 oz/250 g/generous 1 cup
    mascarpone cheese
7 fl oz/200 ml/generous
    ³/₄ cup strained plain yogurt
1 tsp ground ginger
grated rind and juice of 1 lime
2 tbsp soft light brown sugar
8 tbsp raw brown sugar

method

1 Slice the mangoes on either side of the pit. Discard the pit and peel the fruit. Slice and then chop the fruit. Divide it among 4 ramekins.

2 Beat the mascarpone cheese with the yogurt. Fold in the ginger, lime rind and juice, and soft brown sugar. Divide the mixture among the ramekins and level off the tops. Chill for 2 hours.

3 Sprinkle 2 tablespoons of raw brown sugar over the top of each dish, covering the creamy mixture. Place under a hot broiler for 2–3 minutes, until melted and browned. Let cool, then chill until needed. This dessert should be eaten on the day it is made.

mascarpone creams

ingredients

serves 4

4 oz/115 g Amaretti cookies,
    crushed
4 tbsp Amaretto or Maraschino
4 eggs, separated
2 oz/55 g/generous ¼ cup
    superfine sugar
8 oz/225 g/1 cup Mascarpone
    cheese
toasted slivered almonds,
    to decorate

method

1 Place the Amaretti crumbs in a bowl, add the Amaretto or Maraschino, and set aside to soak.

2 Meanwhile, beat the egg yolks with the superfine sugar until pale and thick. Fold in the Mascarpone and soaked cookie crumbs.

3 Whisk the egg whites in a separate, spotlessly clean bowl until stiff, then gently fold into the cheese mixture. Divide the Mascarpone cream among 4 serving dishes and let chill for 1–2 hours. Sprinkle with toasted slivered almonds just before serving.

creamy chocolate dessert

ingredients

serves 4–6

6 oz/175 g semisweet chocolate,
  at least 70% cocoa solids,
  broken up
1½ tbsp orange juice
3 tbsp water
2 tbsp unsalted butter, diced
2 eggs, separated
⅛ tsp cream of tartar
3 tbsp superfine sugar
6 tbsp heavy cream

pistachio-orange praline
corn oil, for greasing
2 oz/55 g/generous ¼ cup
  superfine sugar
2 oz/55 g/scant ½ cup shelled
  pistachios
finely grated rind of 1 large orange

method

1 Melt the chocolate with the orange juice and water
  in a small pan over very low heat, stirring constantly.
  Remove from the heat and melt in the butter until
  incorporated. Scrape the chocolate into a bowl. Beat
  the egg yolks until blended, then beat them into the
  chocolate mixture. Set aside to cool.

2 In a clean bowl, whisk the egg whites with the cream of
  tartar until soft peaks form. Gradually beat in the sugar,
  1 tablespoon at a time, beating well, until the meringue
  is glossy. Beat 1 tablespoon of the meringue mixture
  into the chocolate mixture, then fold in the rest.

3 In a separate bowl, whip the cream until soft peaks
  form. Fold into the chocolate mixture. Spoon into
  individual glass bowls or wine glasses, or 1 large
  serving bowl. Cover with plastic wrap and let chill for
  at least 4 hours.

4 To make the praline, lightly grease a cookie sheet with
  corn oil and set aside. Put the sugar and pistachios in
  a small pan over medium heat. When the sugar starts
  to melt, stir gently until a liquid caramel forms and the
  nuts start popping. Pour the praline onto the cookie
  sheet and finely grate the orange rind over. Let cool
  until firm then coarsely chop. Just before serving,
  sprinkle the praline over the chocolate pudding.

summer dessert

ingredients

serves 6

1 lb 8 oz/675 g mixed soft fruits, such as red currants, black currants, raspberries, and blackberries
5 oz/140 g superfine sugar
2 tbsp crème de framboise liqueur (optional)
6–8 slices of good day-old white bread, crusts removed
heavy cream, to serve

method

1 Place the fruits in a large pan with the sugar. Over low heat, very slowly bring to a boil, stirring carefully to ensure that the sugar has dissolved. Cook over low heat for only 2–3 minutes, until the juices run but the fruit still holds its shape. Add the liqueur if using.

2 Line a 28-fl oz/875-ml/3^1/$_2$-cup pudding bowl with some of the slices of bread (cut them to shape so that the bread fits well). Spoon in the cooked fruit and juices, reserving a little of the juice for later.

3 Cover the surface of the fruit with the remaining bread. Place a plate on top of the pudding and weight it down for at least 8 hours or overnight, while keeping it cool in the refrigerator.

4 Turn out the pudding and pour over the reserved juices to color any white bits of bread that may still be showing. Serve with the heavy cream.

baked apricots with honey

ingredients

serves 2

butter, for greasing
4 apricots, each cut in half
    and pitted
4 tbsp slivered almonds
4 tbsp honey
pinch ground ginger or grated
    nutmeg

method

1 Lightly butter an ovenproof dish large enough to hold the apricot halves in a single layer.

2 Arrange the apricot halves in the dish, cut side up. Sprinkle with the almonds and drizzle the honey over. Dust with the spice.

3 Bake in a preheated oven, 400°F/200°C, for 12–15 minutes until the apricots are tender and the almonds golden. Remove from the oven and serve at once.

banana toffee pies

ingredients

serves 4

two cans sweetened condensed
   milk, about 14 fl oz/400 ml
   each
6 tbsp butter, melted
5½ oz/150 g graham crackers,
   crushed into crumbs
1¾ oz/50 g/⅓ cup almonds,
   toasted and ground
1¾ oz/50 g/⅓ cup hazelnuts,
   toasted and ground
4 ripe bananas
1 tbsp lemon juice
1 tsp vanilla extract
2¾ oz/75 g chocolate flakes
16 fl oz/450 ml/scant 2 cups thick
   heavy cream, whipped

method

1 Place the cans of milk in a large pan and cover them
with water. Bring to a boil, then reduce the heat and let
simmer for 2 hours, topping up the water level regularly
to keep the cans covered. Carefully lift out the hot cans
and let cool.

2 Grease 4 individual loose-bottom tartlet pans with
butter. Put the remaining butter into a bowl and add
the crackers and nuts. Mix together well, then press the
mixture evenly into the bottom of the tartlet pans. Bake
in a preheated oven, 350°F/180°C, for 10–12 minutes,
then remove from the oven and let cool.

3 Open the cans of condensed milk and spread the
contents over the cracker layer in the tartlet pans.
Peel and slice the bananas and put them into a bowl.
Sprinkle over the lemon juice and vanilla extract and
mix gently. Spoon the banana mixture on to the
condensed milk layer, then top with a dollop of
whipped cream. Break up the chocolate flakes, scatter
over the tartlets, and serve.

blueberry filo tart

ingredients

serves 2

4 sheets of filo pastry
rapeseed or vegetable oil spray
7 oz/200 g/1 cup Mascarpone
    cheese
1 tsp honey
1 tbsp finely grated lemon rind
3 tbsp lemon juice
1 tsp superfine sugar
3½ oz/100 g fresh blueberries

method

1 Using a plate as a guide, cut out 4 x 5½-inch/14-cm circles of filo pastry (you need two circles per tartlet). Spray each lightly with oil before laying two circles into 2 x 4-inch/10-cm fluted tartlet pans, pressing the pastry into the corners. Prick the bases with a fork.

2 Put a ramekin into the center of each tartlet shell to prevent the pastry rising, then bake in a preheated oven, 350°F/180°C, for 5 minutes. Remove the ramekins and bake the cases for an additional 4–5 minutes so that the bases cook. Remove from the oven and leave the shells to cool in the tins. Store the cases in an airtight tin so that they remain crisp.

3 Mix the Mascarpone cheese with the honey in a small bowl.

4 Put the lemon rind and juice and the sugar in a small pan over low heat and heat until the liquid has evaporated, then add the blueberries. Stir with a metal spoon to coat the berries in the syrup. Remove from the heat and keep warm.

5 To serve, place each tartlet shell on a serving plate, add a spoonful of the Mascarpone mixture, then spoon over the warmed blueberries.

index